CLASSIC GUITAR

Mel Bay Presents

MELODY & HARMONY FOR GUITARISTS

by John Duarte

MW00784649

Table of Contents

Acknowledgements 2
Foreword.. 3
Musical Sounds and their Organizaton 4
The Organization of Single Notes 9
Melody 29
Intervals 47
The Beginnings of Harmony – Triads 49
Functional Harmony and Cadences............................ 59
Primary Triads and Harmonization............................. 66
Secondary Triads and Substitution............................. 75
Modulation and Transition....................................... 81
Secondary Sevenths... 89
Other Diatonic Secondary Sevenths 97

The Cadential Six-four 100
The Dominant Ninth.. 103
Secondary Ninths... 106
Chords of the Eleventh and Thirteenth...................... 110
Chromatic Alteration of Diatonic Chords 115
Chromatic Harmony 120
Remote Modulation... 131
Pedal Points... 134
Steps Beyond.. 137
Appendix I   Music Quoted In Examples In Text ... 150
Appendix II   Key to Musical Examples 154
Appendix III   Further Reading................................. 158
Index 159

Presented By:

KILGORE MEMORIAL LIBRARY FOUNDATION
MILDRED McCLOUD BEQUEST

ALL RIG... ... PRINTED IN U.S.A.
No part of thi... ..., or transmitted in any form
or by any me... ...ermission of the publisher.

Visit us on the Web at www.melbay.com — E-mail us at email@melbay.com

KILGORE MEMORIAL LIBRARY YORK, NE 68467

Acknowledgements

Thanks are due to the following for permission to reproduce quotations from musical works:

Bèrben: Absil – 1711; Badings – 1641; Batchelar arr. Duarte – 1592; L. Berkeley – 1643; Blyton 1712; Castelnuovo-Tedesco – 1701, 1703, 1704; L. & F. Couperin arr. Duarte – 1844; Crema arr. Duarte – 2122; J. Dowland arr. Duarte – 1592, 1820, 1935, 2015, 2121; Duarte – 1419, 1514, 1520, 1971, 1972, 2042, 2043; Fox – 1644; Haug – 1480; Holborne arr. Duarte – 1725; Morley arr. Duarte – 2090; Rosetta - 1719, 1720, 1813; Santorsola – 1722; Schubert arr. Duarte – 1819; Stoker – 1978; Wissmer – 1518

Broekmans & Van Poppel: Duarte – 1015; Weiss arr. Duarte – 1286

Columbia Music Company: Duarte – 1530, 183; Tórroba – 1680

Ediciones Joaquin Rodrigo: Rodrigo 190127

Eschig: Duarte – 8213; Filippi – Galliarde; Pujol – 1204; Villa-Lobos – Preludes 2, 3 & 5

Faber Music: Britten – Nocturnal Op. 70

Novello & Co. Ltd: Beethoven arr. Choppen – Andante, Op. 14/2; L. Couperin arr. Duarte – three of Six Pieces; Duarte – English Suite Op. 31, Six Easy Pictures Op. 56, Sonatinette Op. 35, Variations on a Catalan Folksong Op. 25

Oxford University Press: Dodgson – Partita

Ricordi: Duarte – Some of Noah's Ark, LD 583; Sor – Sonata Op. 25, BA 9600; Wills – Pavane and Galliard, LD 615

G. Schirmer: Norman – Exit, 45408

Schott & Co. Ltd: Aguado – GA 62; J.S. Bach – GA 213/214; Brouwer – GA 423; Castelnuovo-Tedesco – GA 149; Coste – GA 12; Farnaby – 10988; Franck – GA 118; Frescobaldi – GA 158; Handel – GA 148; Haydn – GA 139; Legnani – GA 74; Mozart – GA 117; Mudarra and Narvaez – GA 176; Pedrell – GA 120; Ponce – GA 109, 110, 122, 123, 124, 125, 135, 151, 153; Rameau – GA 160; Ravel – GA 494; Scarlatti – GA 228; Tansman – GA 165, 206; Tórroba – GA 103, 104, 113, 115, 134; Turina – GA 102, 128, 136; Two minuets from 11081 (A Grace of Minuets)

Suvini Zerboni: Castelnuovo-Tedesco – 6725, 6854; Giuliani – 7727, 7764; Milan – complete vihuela works; Milano – complete lute works; Sor – 7890; Spinacino – 6892; Weiss – complete works from British Museum.

Tuscany Publications: Duarte – Birds Op. 66

Universal Edition (London) Ltd: 11461, 13942, 14463, 29153, 29157, works by Edward Collard & Esaias Reusner

Zanibon: Cammarota – 5262; Dowland arr. Duarte – 5579

Zimmermann: Fink – 1835

Foreword

INTRODUCTION

In learning the language of music the guitarist is in a position that is both strong and uniquely difficult, though the problems are partially shared by harpists. The ability of the guitar to express harmony is matched only by that of the keyboard and harp, in comparison with which it has both advantages and limitations. The harmony examples given in standard textbooks are, however, laid out for the keyboard, which is additionally studied by players of other instruments. The guitarist must first translate these into fingerboard terms, a task few students can perform without disproportionate labour. Such work is beneficial in itself, but it retards the attainment of the primary objective – the understanding of musical content. Further, the examples given are, where not simply devised to illustrate some particular point, not drawn from guitar music; the guitarist must make a personal search in order to relate the knowledge gained to the actual instrument. Students in even the highest educational establishments are seldom in any better position than those working in private. A very high proportion of the examples in this book are drawn from the music of the guitar and its ancestors; the remainder are set out in forms directly playable on the guitar.

The primary aim of this book is to help the reader to understand the language of music, and how it works in relation to the guitar. It is *not* intended as a substitute for all other lines of study, but it will provide a basic knowledge that can be expanded and developed. The reader is urged to read as wide a range of books as possible, and to examine whatever music he or she possesses to identify further examples of the points discussed. The examples should be *played and carefully listened to*. The study of music is sterile if confined to making marks on paper, no matter how well understood intellectually; no real value attaches to a theoretical study of music unless it is directly related to aural experience, and its value is reduced further if it is not related to the music of one's instrument.

Melody and harmony are studied together because, at least for the guitarist, it is difficult to hear a melody without clothing it in the mind with simple harmony, and to hear a succession of chords without associating them with melody. The study of disembodied harmony, even when it does not descend to the absurd depths of the 'chordal encyclopedia', is futile. This book makes no claim to have solved the problems inherent in a combined approach, but it is written with an awareness that they exist. It is assumed that the reader is already acquainted with the rudiments of music – correct notation, formation of scales, composition and naming of intervals etc. – and these are not discussed here, since other, reliable books on the subject are available, including *The Guitarist's ABC of Music* by the present author (Novello). Suggestions for further reading are given in Appendix III.

John W. Duarte (2004)

Musical Sounds and their Organization

Music consists of organized successions of sounds used singly and in simultaneous combinations. We begin by considering the single musical sound from which everything else develops. There are sounds of many kinds, some of which we describe loosely as 'musical', others as 'non-musical'. Non-musical sounds have always been used as an adjunct to music, for example those made by various percussion instruments, but in the last century the distinction became less sharp since, in some forms of music, for example musique concrète, non-musical sounds such as pistol shots and traffic noises were used as an integral part of the 'musical' fabric itself. Nevertheless our broad concept of what is musical and what is not remains essentially the same; most of the music enjoyed by most people is still firmly based on musical sounds.

VIBRATION

When any object moves to and fro rapidly enough, i.e. vibrates, it sets up waves of fluctuating pressure in the surrounding air, and these are detected by the ear. One complete to-and-fro motion is called a cycle:

= one cycle

A musical sound is produced by regular vibration, i.e. one which performs the same number of cycles in each second of its life; such vibration is termed **oscillation**. The pitch of a sound (its highness or lowness) depends only on the frequency of the oscillation, i.e. how many cycles it completes in each second (c.p.s.), and *not* on the nature of the vibrating body. Thus, providing they all oscillate with the same frequency, a nylon string, an air-column (for example in a flute), a block of wood or a strip of metal, will all give the same pitch. The higher the frequency the higher the pitch of the resulting note. The width of the oscillation, i.e. how far the vibrating body moves away from its rest position, is described as the **amplitude**: and it determines the loudness of the note. Thus, at the beginning of its life, a note may be loud – corresponding to a wide and vigorous motion – and may then die away into silence as the amplitude decreases and eventually becomes zero. Throughout, the frequency will remain exactly the same, a certain number of journeys per second, the journeys becoming shorter as the sound dies away. Irregular vibrations produce non-musical sounds of indefinite or unstable pitch. We will now concentrate on the vibration (or oscillation) of strings, which are easier to visualize (one cannot see an air-column, for instance) and are also the basis of our own instrument, the guitar.

THE VIBRATION OF STRINGS

When a string vibrates, the pitch of the note it gives depends on three characteristics of the string itself: (i) length, (ii) tension, (iii) weight. For any given string (i.e. the weight does not change), if the length remains the same, pitch rises as tension increases; we use this fact when tuning the instrument. Once the string is tuned and its tension therefore fixed, the shorter the string is made the higher will be the note it gives: this is what happens when the string is pressed against a fret. Of two strings of the same length and under equal tension, the heavier one will give the lower note; string manufacturers use this fact to ensure that all six strings present about the same resistance to our left-hand fingers.

The fifth string of the guitar sounds the note A below middle C (in terms of guitar notation) and this corresponds to a vibration of the following type:

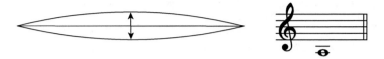

If the string is lightly touched at the twelfth fret, exactly halfway along its length, it will sound a note one octave higher than before and the string, now unable to move at its midpoint, vibrates like two strings, each half the length of the original one:

This higher note is known as a **harmonic**; it is also variously known as a **partial** (since the string vibrates in 'parts'), or an **overtone** (because it is higher than the original note, termed the **fundamental** – given when the string vibrates as a whole). These terms are mildly confusing since, for reasons that will become clear in time, the fundamental is known as the first overtone, harmonic or partial! The octave note is thus the *second* overtone. The points where the string must remain still are termed **nodes** – there are always at least two, since the string is anchored at both ends; those where its movement is greatest are called **loops**:

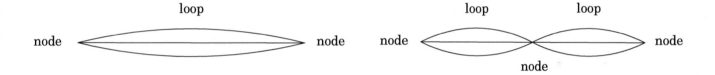

Thus, when the length of a string is halved, its sounding pitch is raised by an octave and, in fact, its frequency is doubled. The general rule is that the frequency of the note is inversely proportional to the length of the string – half the length, double the frequency, one third of the length, treble the frequency, and so on. If the string is touched at the seventh fret, one-third of the way along its length, an even higher harmonic (the third) results, easily identified as the E above the previous (octave) A. The mode of vibration is now:

The third harmonic is thus a perfect fifth above the second, and a perfect fifth corresponds to a frequency ratio of 3:2.

A series of higher notes (overtones) may be obtained by touching the string at integral fractions of its length – 1/4, 1/5, 1/6, 1/7 etc. – giving what is known as the **overtone series**, a progression of notes derived from the natural behaviour of the string itself. In this way we can derive a series of related notes from Nature herself; ironically we shall soon find ourselves at variance with Nature, unwilling to accept what she offers.

Since every possible frequency corresponds to a different note there are clearly infinite possibilities, even within the range of frequencies the human ear can detect. This range varies with the hearer, his/her age and state of health, but is still *much* smaller than the range that is possible in fact; for dogs it is said to be somewhat wider. We have selected a comparatively small number of these possible notes for our use in Western music-making and have given them names – twelve in all, plus their octave recurrences. The question arises as to the frequencies we have selected; whatever these may be they are clearly related to one another, and all are fixed when any one is fixed. For example, the exact pitches of a series of overtones depend on that of the fundamental, though their relationships to one another remain the same.

In earlier times the pitch we have used has been so variable that the term 'standard' would be a misnomer. On the whole it has tended to rise, so that Beethoven's 'middle C' was a little higher than Bach's, but a little lower than it is now. In the Renaissance, however, though some instruments were tuned to even lower pitches, there were also organs tuned to pitches higher than those we use today. The contemporary directive to lutenists to tune the first string as high as they felt safe and then to tune the others to it makes nonsense of any suggestion of standard pitch at those times. There is *still* no one standard pitch to which everyone adheres, though a 'concert pitch' (A above middle C = 440 c.p.s.) was agreed internationally in 1939 and is now used under most conditions. Any good musical encyclopedia will give fuller information on this far-from-simple matter. Once the pitch of *any* one note is specified, that of all others is automatically determined; it is a question of relationships.

THE NOTES OF MUSIC

Two basic relationships have emerged from our simple study of the string as a typical vibrating body:

1. A frequency ratio of 2:1 represents an octave.

2. A frequency ratio of 3:2 corresponds to a perfect fifth.

The first merely leads to octaves of the same note, but the second opens a gateway to new territory. In noting this we are following in the steps of Pythagoras (6th century B.C.), though he recognized it in terms of string-length and not frequency, which is a more modern concept. As a 'classical' Greek he had deep respect for the beauty and fundamental truth of simple, mathematical relationships, and there is none simpler than 2:3, other than 1:2 – which, applied to musical notes, leads only to octaves. We may follow his lead, repeatedly using 3:2 from a starting note and therefore, in twentieth-century language, making a pile of perfect fifths. Starting from C:

$$C - G - D - A - E - B - F\sharp - C\sharp - G\sharp - D\sharp - A\sharp - E\sharp - B\sharp$$

at which stage we seem to have come full circle, since B♯ *is* C, enharmonically speaking. We might however have worked in reverse, using a 2:3 ratio, and thus *descending* each time by a perfect fifth:

C - F - B♭ - E♭ - A♭ - D♭ - G♭ - C♭ - F♭ - B♭♭ - E♭♭ - A♭♭ - D♭♭

and again we arrive at an enharmonic form of C, that is, D♭♭. By this means we have derived every one of the twelve notes into which we now subdivide the octave, plus a few enharmonic forms of them. Unfortunately, all is less well than it seems. If we were to calculate the frequency given by multiplying the starting frequency by $(3/2)^{12}$, and then return it to the same pitch by using the 1:2 ratio as many times as necessary to regain the original octave, we should find B♯ a little higher in pitch than the C from which we began; a similar exercise would also show that D♭♭ is a fraction lower, so that our journey is not truly 'circular'. It did in fact commence a sort of Swiss roll that would be further developed if we continued beyond the twelve steps taken in each direction, piling up sharps and flats *ad lib*:

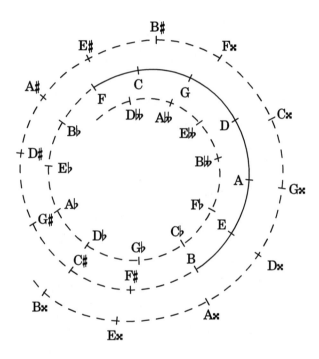

The pitch-difference between these apparent enharmonic notes, small but easily audible, is termed the 'comma of Pythagoras'.

These discrepancies did not matter much while music was in the early stages of its development, since situations did not arise in which they would have caused discomfort through 'out-of-tuneness'. The earliest music was essentially monophonic in character, and vocal rather than instrumental; for some time after, it remained 'unadventurous' enough to avoid serious problems arising, for instance, from any conflict between C♯ and D♭. With the rapid development of music in general, and keyboard music in particular, problems became increasingly acute.

7

If we accept the pitches of notes Nature gives to us then we acknowledge also that enharmonic notes do *not* share exactly the same pitch. While some instruments, for example the bowed-string family and the trombone, can play notes of *any* pitch within their compass, others cannot; in tuning a keyboard instrument, building a keyed wind instrument, or placing the frets on a guitar, one has to decide on the exact pitch of each note. Is it to be C♯ or D♭? It is physically impracticable to have both: this was, and still remains, the essence of the problem. Nature gives us all the notes we require to fill our octave but, whether derived as above or taken from the higher harmonics of a vibrating body, we have been unable to come to terms with them in music as it has developed smoothly during the last 400 years. The Pythagorean comma, small as it is (about a quarter of a semitone), has continued to haunt our attempts at musical perfection.

At first, various efforts were made to minimize the difficulties by slight alterations to the tuning of certain notes – rather like building a strong, national defence by protecting only the borders of the land itself. It is beyond the scope of this book to discuss this matter further; there are many good accounts of these early experiments in musical encyclopedias. In his book *The Craft of Musical Composition* (Schott) Paul Hindemith discussed the problems of arriving at satisfactory tunings. The further music has progressed, the more it has become obvious that efforts to cling to such 'pure' forms of tuning were doomed to failure.

To put it simply, if we arrange the 'natural' notes in chromatic order within an octave, we will find that, whichever enharmonics we choose, the notes are not spaced equally: i.e., 'semitone' steps are not equal and two 'semitones' do not add up to one 'whole-tone'. The advantages of bringing enharmonic notes to one common pitch, so that the twelve semitones within the octave are of equal size, are obvious. However, to do this we have to change, in different degrees, the pitch of every note except for the two that enclose the octave itself. This slightly mars the perfection of even the fifth, and the result sounds out-of-tune to an ear accustomed to hearing the notes at their 'natural' pitches. *Any* system of tuning the notes of music is called **temperament**, and that by which all semitones are made equal is called **equal temperament**. There is evidence that, even two centuries before the birth of Bach (1685), composers thought in terms of possible equal temperament, and some instruments, including guitars, were made in keeping with it. Evidently it was not accepted by musicians in general, however, and it was not until Bach advocated its use, and wrote the Forty-eight preludes and fugues (BWV 846–893), showing that the system made it possible to be equally uncomfortable in all keys, that the tide turned in its favour. This system of tuning is now almost universally used, though organ-builders resisted it until 1851 at least. We are now so thoroughly accustomed to this system that we tend to think of it as 'the way it has always been'; to our ears, natural or compromise forms of temperament now seem out-of-tune, though some harpsichord recordings now give us the opportunity to adjust to them and to hear the music as the composer did. Most early fretted instruments had moveable frets to allow for adjustment of intonation to suit the music in hand. The fixed frets of today's guitars reflect our acceptance of equal temperament; our difficulties in arriving at a tuning that is satisfactory within all keys show that problems in this area still remain.

We now use, therefore, an octave divided into twelve equal semitone steps, and we take our bearings on the establishment of 440 c.p.s. for the A above middle C. These are the basic raw materials of our music.

The Organization of Single Notes

Of the three basic ingredients of Western music, rhythm is the most primitive and was probably the first to attract the attention of early man; melody is the next in importance, and it dominated pitched music for many centuries before the appearance of the third, and most sophisticated: harmony. While the dawn of music was attended by the discovery of tunes rather than the pursuit of theories, there is evidence that thoughts about some kind of organization of the notes came at an early stage. Pythagoras studied the relationships between notes and defined a system for their arrangement in 'families', one that dominated music until about 400 years ago and thus had a life of more than 2000 years; as these 'families' are still used, their effective life cannot yet be said to be ended.

In the arts, not least in music, theory *follows* practice and is in fact arrived at by examining the best of what has been done, in search of discernible guidelines; these become 'rules' or 'laws' and apply strictly (and none too strictly at that) only to music of and before the time in which they were formulated. Progress has always resulted from the calculated breaking of rules and the eventual acceptance of their 'infringement' – what would have shocked Grandma is today's commonplace, and it has always been so. New paths in music have always been taken as a result of instinctive action rather than the working out of some new theory, though the twentieth century has seen changes in this field, as in many others. First we will see what is to be learned of the musical families, from the melodies that doubtless came first.

If we examine some traditional melodies we can determine which notes they contain, extract these and place them in some kind of order. It is a basic human instinct to put things into order, and that of ascending pitch is as logical as any for a group of notes. We may also feel that the last note of a melody, with its responsibility of establishing a sense of finality, has special importance. We may therefore begin and end a family of notes with it. Exs. 1a–d yield clear families of seven notes:

Ex. 1a

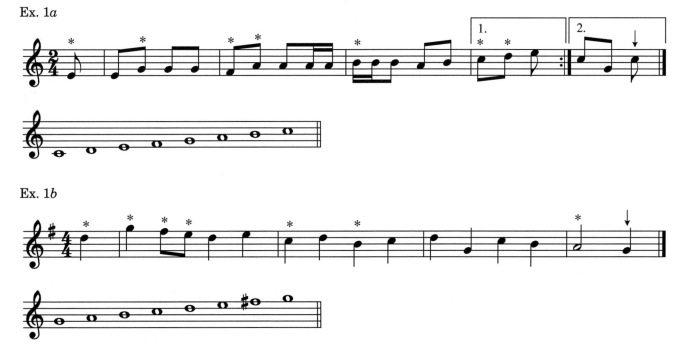

Ex. 1b

Ex. 1c

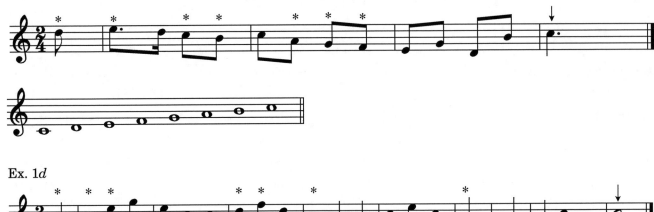

Ex. 1d

If we look upon a seven-note group as the norm then Exs. 1e and f are incomplete (the bracketed notes are in the unshown parts of the tunes) but they fall neatly into line with the complete ones. All the notes of 1e belong to the same family group as that of Exs. 1a, c and d, while those of Ex. 1f find their place in the wider context of Ex. 1b. The missing members are simply having a day off.

Ex. 1e

Ex. 1f

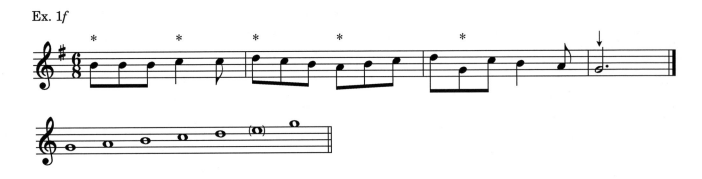

10

There are many kinds of family group of this nature, with seven notes, known as **heptatonic scales**. In the earlier history of music there have been (and in some parts of the world still are) groups containing less than seven notes, called **gapped scales**; the word 'scale' signifies a ladder of sounds, with the gaps corresponding to missing rungs. Some primitive peoples still use scales of only two notes, just enough to avoid total monotony, but the best-known gapped scale is the **pentatonic scale**, the basis of much Gaelic music, for example bag-pipe music. Ex. 2*a* shows this, and 2*b* gives one example of a Scottish tune using this scale; it is easy to find others.

Ex. 2*a*   Pentatonic scale

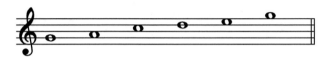

Ex. 2*b*

The scales derived from Exs. 1*e* and *f* are not gapped but incompletely used within the tunes concerned. We now refer to the family groups of notes as 'scales', which is exactly what they are.

The scale extracted from Ex. 3 contains all the notes of Ex. 1*b* (there is an F♯ in the omitted part of the tune), but also a few C♯s. These latter are subsidiary in both placing and effect and if, in playing the tune, one replaces them with a C♮ or even a D, one realizes how small is their effect on the tune as a whole; they merely smooth its passage, and we may look on them as visiting friends of the family and not members of it:

Ex. 3

Apply the above method to other, similar tunes – popular music usually springs from the grassroots. You will find similar results many times over. Some will not fit into any of the patterns we have discovered, but we shall come to these in due course.

SCALES – THE FAMILY GROUPS

We have extracted two different families of notes, one starting and finishing on C, the other on G. If we play them one after the other we can hear their close family resemblance, even though they do not use exactly the same notes; they sound like different versions of the same thing. In fact they share six common notes and may be thought of as blood-related families. Each is immediately recognizable as what we know as a **major scale** and, had we started the tunes on different notes, we would have discovered further major scales. Here we have reversed the usual process, deriving the scales from melodies whose raw material they are. This is closer to historical truth and it places the horse in front of the cart, where it belongs.

The most important feature of the major or any other type of scale is that it represents a family with a clearly established head, the **tonic**, the note from which so many tunes start and to which the great majority return at their end. We can view the diatonic scales, of which the major scale is the most important, as organizations which, like their domestic, national, political or commercial counterparts, have their overall head – father, king, chairman, president or the like. The other members have defined tasks within the organization and firm relationships with the head – mother, princess, manager, treasurer, foreign minister, charge-hand and so on. If we play any selection of major scales in succession, we hear them as different ways of saying the same thing; all have the same pattern of sound:

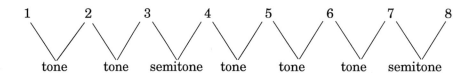

This common pattern, expressive of the special relationships within the major-scale family, is one we recognize by its sound, and understand in terms of its interval succession; we can also *see* it on the guitar. Any 'moveable' major-scale fingering, i.e. one that may be played at any fret within reach, exhibits this pattern in terms of the instrument itself. Thus, beginning at the third fret on the sixth string, it yields G major; from the fourth fret it gives A♭ major, and from the seventh, B major:

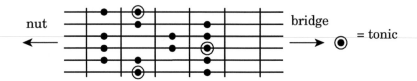

The visual evidence that all major scales form essentially the same pattern operating at different levels is very clear on the guitar. It is not so on the keyboard, where every scale has its individual succession of black and white keys, nor even with the guitar when it is taught in the usual way – beginning in the nut position where each scale has a different appearance on the fingerboard.

Each degree of a scale has its own special function, and it is the same in all heptatonic scales. A filing clerk is a filing clerk in *any* office, the dominant remains the dominant in *any* key or scale. Personal or note names are 'trivial' and refer to those concerned and not to the jobs they do. It is possible, for instance, to work in a factory and simply to identify the manager, foreman, cashier, etc., without knowing their names: in another factory their functions would be the same but their names probably different. If we do not have 'perfect pitch' we can still recognize the dominant, mediant or leading note, for example, by their sound, once we have got our bearings from the relevant scale or tonic note. If you cannot do this, practise daily, playing any major scale, and then, separately, any of its notes, listening objectively and relating the sound to that of the scale as a whole. Do this until you are confident you can recognize which degree of the scale you are hearing. Then learn to do the same, but playing only the tonic note to begin with, followed by the other, varying degree. In both stages the detached note should, ideally, be unknown, but it is difficult to give oneself an 'unseen' of this kind; at such times there is no substitute for a co-operative friend.

CHANGING KEY

There are many circumstances under which one might wish to change the key of a piece of music or of part of it. One that recurs frequently is in adapting music for the guitar, to change the original key to one more suited to the instrument. The process of changing key is, in this context, termed **transposition**. What we have learned about musical patterns, and the fact that function is much more important than trivial name, will help us to transpose easily and as a natural outcome of our knowledge.

Each note in the original key has its function within the scale of that key, whether it appears within the scale or in a piece of music; the corresponding note in the new key will naturally have the same function in that new key. The tonic note in the original key will obviously be replaced by the tonic note in the second; likewise for every other degree. We can make a chart in which all the notes of the normally used major keys are written, above one another and in chromatic order (for easy reference) so that the tonics form one vertical column, the dominants another, and so on.

C	D	E	F	G	A	B	C
D♭	E♭	F	G♭	A♭	B♭	C	D♭
D	E	F♯	G	A	B	C♯	D
E♭	F	G	A♭	B♭	C	D	E♭
E	F♯	G♯	A	B	C♯	D♯	E
F	G	A	B♭	C	D	E	F
F♯	G♯	A♯	B	C♯	D♯	E♯	F♯
G♭	A♭	B♭	C♭	D♭	E♭	F	G♭
G	A	B	C	D	E	F♯	G
A♭	B♭	C	D♭	E♭	F	G	A♭
A	B	C♯	D	E	F♯	G♯	A
B♭	C	D	E♭	F	G	A	B♭
B	C♯	D♯	E	F♯	G♯	A♯	B

Ex. 4 shows a simple melody in C major, to be transposed to F major. Our starting point is the horizontal line of C major, our objective is that of F major. The first note, C, obviously becomes F in the new situation. The next is G in the key of C, so we locate it in the C major line and look down the vertical column until we come to the F major line, where we find the corresponding note to be C (also the dominant of its key). The process is repeated for each note in turn and, of course, the new notes will reproduce the outline of the original tune.

Ex. 5 shows the transfer from one key/scale to the other, the numbering showing the order in which the notes are met in working through Ex. 4:

Ex. 4

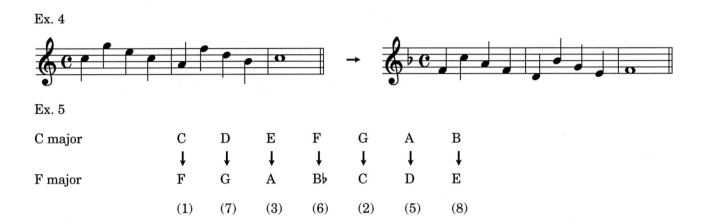

Ex. 5

C major		C	D	E	F	G	A	B
		↓	↓	↓	↓	↓	↓	↓
F major		F	G	A	B♭	C	D	E
		(1)	(7)	(3)	(6)	(2)	(5)	(8)

The transposition of chromatically altered notes is simple. In Ex. 6 there are several of these; each is first transposed by letter-name only and then chromatically changed in the same direction and by the same amount as the note in the original. In choosing our starting line on the chart we are guided by the *key signature*, not the identity of the key itself. Ex. 6 is in a minor key and would be laborious to transpose from a base of A, so we begin on the C major line (same key signature). Ex. 7 shows the transfers of the chromatically inflected notes only to the new base of E (minor), the complete transposition being shown in Ex. 6 itself. Had we transposed the tune into D minor (= F major) the first chromatic change would have been to B♮, as in Ex. 7*a*. Transpose Exs. 4 and 6 into several other keys as an exercise.

Ex. 6

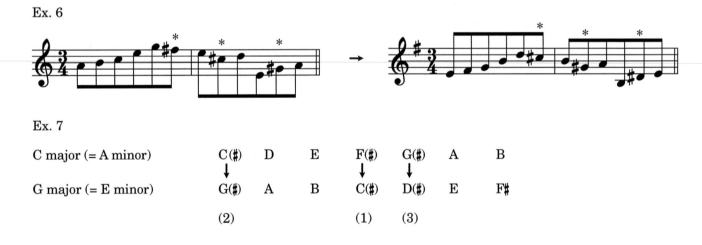

Ex. 7

C major (= A minor)		C(♯)	D	E	F(♯)	G(♯)	A	B
		↓			↓	↓		
G major (= E minor)		G(♯)	A	B	C(♯)	D(♯)	E	F♯
		(2)			(1)	(3)		

Ex. 7*a*

To summarize: transposition from one major key to another is a simple matter of 'trading' between the two scales. As so many forms of minor scale are in common use it is futile to make a parallel working chart from them; instead we use the notes of the relative major scales, choosing by key signature. Chromatically changed notes are first treated as though they were normal scale degrees and then chromatically inflected to match those in the original key. There are many ways to transpose but none simpler to understand or to use; neither is any so clearly based on the fact that notes have the same function in all keys. Provided no open string is used, it is necessary only to play a melody on the guitar, moving the fingering pattern to a higher or lower position, in order to 'transpose' it.

OTHER SCALES

The major scale has occupied a position of prime importance in the Western music of the last four or five centuries, but it is by no means the only scale to have been used widely. Broadly speaking it is one of the family of **diatonic scales**, that is, those having each alphabet letter once only, no matter how inflected. Diatonic scales subdivide into major or minor, according to whether the interval between tonic and mediant is a major or minor third. By textbook definition there are three types of minor scale – harmonic, melodic ascending and melodic descending – but the distinction is largely artificial and is persistently contradicted in musical practice. When the course of a melody results in the need for a major harmony where, in theory, a minor might have been expected, this is often explained by using terms such as 'borrowing' from the major. While minor scales are highly important and are loosely regarded as being of equal status with major ones, the minor scale is not a clearly defined entity and lacks, in all its forms, the symmetrical strength and adaptability of the major. How this situation has come about is no simple matter, nor is it fully explicable, but we can gain some insight by considering earlier forms of diatonic scale.

THE MODES

Our present system of major and minor scales has been firmly established for no more than 400 years, and before that another group of diatonic scales dominated music for a far longer period. In constructing major scales we use the concept of the tetrachord, a diatonic succession of four notes; by definition there are many kinds of tetrachord. On logical bases beyond the scope of this book, Pythagoras devised a system of tetrachords of different compositions – the 'major' form of tone-tone-semitone was one of those he described.

The birth of music as we know it was in the hymns and plainchants of the early Christians. When, in 146 B.C., the Roman Empire conquered and swallowed up Greece, it was at the same time itself 'conquered' by more peaceful means. The Romans, having no worthwhile culture and music of their own, gradually adopted that of the captive Greeks, including their system of scales termed *modes*. As Christianity spread, there grew a corpus of hymns and chants (plainsong), the process being accelerated by the freedom given through the issue of an edict of toleration by Emperor Constantine (274-337 A.D.) in 313 A.D. Plainsong and the modal system developed together, determinative contributions being made by St Ambrosius (340-397 A.D.) and Pope Gregory I (540-604 A.D.), both of whom are remembered in the naming of forms of plainchant used in the Catholic Church, where these ancient forms of music may still be heard, virtually unchanged.

The ancient modes, often referred to as the 'ecclesiastical' or 'church' modes for obvious reasons, were identified by names we believe to have referred to peoples or areas in ancient Greece. In 1547 the Roman theorist Glareanus gave an account, in his treatise *Dodecachordon*, of the modal system as he saw it. He retained the established order of the scales themselves and numbered them in a way we still observe; he also confused their names so that they did not correspond to the original scales. We now refer to the modes by the names Glareanus gave them.

The modes were conceived only as sources of melody, harmony as we understand it being then unknown; this played a part in the ultimate downfall of the system in the seventeenth century.

The simplest way to approach the modes is to recognize that they used only those notes corresponding to the uninflected alphabet letters A-G, and differed according to which of these was the starting note. The modes, with Glareanus' numbers and names, are shown in Ex. 8:

Ex. 8

I	-	D	E	F	G	A	B	C	D	....	Dorian
III	-	E	F	G	A	B	C	D	E	....	Phrygian
V	-	F	G	A	B	C	D	E	F	....	Lydian
VII	-	G	A	B	C	D	E	F	G	....	Mixolydian
IX	-	A	B	C	D	E	F	G	A	....	Aeolian
XI	-	C	D	E	F	G	A	B	C	....	Ionian or Iastian

Each has a different pattern of tones and semitones. The 'home' note was termed the **final** of the mode, on which all modal melodies came to rest, from whatever point they started, and it served the same purpose as today's tonic. Each mode had also its **dominant**, usually its fifth note, as in today's major and minor scales, serving as an alternative focus of interest to that of the final itself; it did not have the special significance it has in the major/minor scale system. The use of variety coupled with return to home ground is at the root of many musical usages, as it is also in ordinary life. Music, like good art, mirrors life itself.

The modal system shown in Ex. 8 has two patent divergences from what one might expect: first, there is no ancient mode starting from B. Such a mode, though theoretically possible, could not have existed in practice, for reasons we shall soon understand, but Roman theorists with tidy minds invented one and called it 'Locrian'. Glareanus rejected this and history has agreed with him, though John Ireland used it at the end of his Fantasy-Sonata for Clarinet and Piano, 1943. Second, only odd-numbered modes are shown; these are termed **authentic modes** and, when they were used, the melody usually stayed within the compass of the octave between two finals. Occasionally a melody would lie between the two dominants, acquiring also a fresh dominant, but would end on the usual final. These forms of the mode, lying below the authentic, were called **plagal modes** (it merely means 'beneath'); they occupy the even numbers and share the same name as the authentic forms, prefixed by 'hypo-'. These, together with the authentic modes, are given in Ex. 9:

BUT : Apply a forceful enough,
mathematical musical pattern !

Ex. 9

I	Dorian				D	E	F	G	A	B	C	D
II	Hypodorian	A	B	C	D	E	F	G	A			
III	Phrygian				E	F	G	A	B	C	D	E
IV	Hypophrygian	B	C	D	E	F	G	A	B			
V	Lydian				F	G	A	B	C	D	E	F
VI	Hypolydian	C	D	E	F	G	A	B	C			
VII	Mixolydian				G	A	B	C	D	E	F	G
VIII	Hypomixolydian	D	E	F	G	A	B	C	D			
IX	Aeolian				A	B	C	D	E	F	G	A
X	Hypoaeolian	E	F	G	A	B	C	D	E			
XI	Ionian				C	D	E	F	G	A	B	C
XII	Hypoionian	G	A	B	C	D	E	F	G			

A melody that stepped widely beyond the compass of an octave was said to be in a **mixed mode**. We have in some ways simplified our account of the modal system, but it will serve our purpose. The reader who wishes to explore the matter more deeply should consult the fuller accounts in textbooks, with the warning that it is, at full stretch, extremely complex and, in some aspects, subject to argument among experts.

Nope. USE it as a matter of chance.

There is an important way in which the modes differ from the major and minor scales we now use. In securing variety, we transpose passages or whole melodies from one key or scale to another; this arises naturally from the identical patterning of major and minor scales beginning on different notes but remaining in the same mode – the term 'mode' here differentiates between major and minor keys sharing the same tonic. In the modal system as it was originally employed, such a practice was unknown. Any one piece of music remained, with few (and often debated) exceptions, in one mode throughout. Hand in hand with this was the fact that each mode was individual in its succession of tones and semitones *and* was regarded as having a distinctive character – as in the **ragas** of Indian classical music. The Dorian mode was considered the most suitable for devotional music while, at the other extreme, Plato (427-387 B.C.) advocated the banning of the Lydian mode from his ideal Republic on the grounds that it was 'licentious'. We may not now be able to hear the modes in this way, but our distant predecessors did.

Some introductory explanation?!?

The finest use of the modes was in sacred music, but the system was also the *lingua franca* of secular music, to a degree not reflected in any twentieth-century idiom. Not all the modes found widespread and international use. Though its use in British folk music was extremely rare, the Phrygian mode is still the basis of true Flamenco, and the Lydian mode was much favoured in Polish folk music. Most of the examples in Ex. 10 are of folk origin, and when they are played they should be listened to as pure melody, not clothed in notional harmony.

Ex. 10a (Dorian)

Ex. 10b (Hypodorian)

Ex. 10c (Phrygian)

Ex. 10d (Hypoaeolian)

Ex. 10e (Mixolydian)

Examples are given in Ex. 11 of their use by renaissance composers, though by then the modes were used for music that was no longer monophonic and the dominant did not play its former role:

Ex. 11a (Dlugoraj)

Dorian, on base of B

Ex. 11b (Bakfark)

Aeolian, on base of B

Ex. 11c (Bakfark)

Phrygian, on base of D

Ex. 11d (Milano)

Mixolydian, on base of D

Ex. 11e (Crema)

Aeolian, on base of E

* (1) see p. 25, para (iv)

* (2) see p. 24, para (iii).

In the last century we resumed the use of modal scales, perhaps feeling that when they were discarded the baby was thrown out with the bath-water. We used them as musical resources in their own right, as alternative forms of scale, and not in the manner for which they were originally conceived. In Ex. 12 there are some examples of the use of modal scales by twentieth-century guitar composers:

Ex. 12*a* (Duarte)

Dorian, on base of G

Ex. 12*b* (Duarte)

Mixolydian, on base of G

Ex. 12*c* (Tansman)

Lydian, on base of G

Ex. 12*d* (Tansman)

Aeolian, on base of A

Ex. 12*e* (Ponce)

Lydian, on base of D

Ex. 12*f* (Tansman)

Dorian, on base of A

Ex. 12*g* (Duarte)

Dorian or Aeolian, on base of D

Ex. 12h (Tansman)

Dorian or Aeolian, on base of D

In fact the modal system never died out completely; many composers, including Bach and Beethoven, wrote works using modal scales, but until the twentieth century examples were sporadic.

In Exs. 12a and b the change in key-signature transforms the mode from Dorian to Mixolydian, a change from a minor mode to the 'tonic' major, bringing about a more cheerful effect at the end of the movement. The taste for the Lydian mode in Polish folk song is reflected in the music of Alexandre Tansman, as shown in c ; the same mode appears in the far-removed music of Manuel Ponce, a Mexican, in e. In his *Suite in modo Polonico* Tansman also uses the Aeolian (d) and Dorian (f) modes; in the latter case the melody ends clearly on the tonic/final even though the harmony is indeterminate. A common factor between g and h is that both melodies have D as tonic but both lack the sixth degree in their melody (despite a key-signature of one flat) so that it is not clear whether they are in the Aeolian (with a B♭) or Dorian (with a B♮); in each case the harmony makes use of both B♭ and B♮, leaving the problem unresolved. It is not important that the question should be answered; scales arise from melodies, not the converse, and it is of melodies that composers think, without conscious effort to use any particular scale. Here the persistent use of a whole-tone leading note proclaims quite clearly *some* form of modal scale.

DECAY OF THE MODES

We may now see what caused the collapse of the long-established modal system and, to begin with, we need do no more than play any major scale, stopping short at the seventh degree, for example C-B. The 'need' to complete it by playing the final C will be apparent. Now, if we play the sequence C D E F G A B♭, we will feel happier when the last C arrives, but the final step feels more permissive than mandatory. This is because a semitone step exerts a stronger 'magnetic' pull and sense of inevitability compared with one of a whole tone. This force of attraction is strong in whichever direction the notes move. Play the Phrygian mode, descending, and hear it as you move from the penultimate note to the final. Rising semitones in such situations are termed **leading notes** (the use in connection with the seventh degree of a scale is only one specific one); those that descend are called **leaning notes**, irrespective of musical context.

This powerful pull of the semitone was sensed by singers and players quite early in musical history and eventually they responded to it, at first only in performance because the Church, whose hand for a long time controlled the highest musical practices, disapproved of such meddling and regarded it as heresy, if not sacrilege. The practice was tolerated providing the changes were not written down, but it eventually became acceptable even on paper. This kind of alteration was known as **musica ficta** ('made' or 'falsified' music). When at last the accidental signs were written they were placed *outside* the staff, above the note concerned; where they lay above two or more notes written as a chord it was commonly *understood* which note they referred to. The accidental was in fact first called a **signum asinorum** (since only an ass would need to be told about it!) Finally, as their use became more widespread, and as the development of music became such as to make misunderstandings possible, accidentals were placed within the staff, next to the note concerned.

If we apply the implications of this change to the modes we arrive at Ex. 13.

Ex. 13

Dorian: melodic minor ascending

Lydian: no change

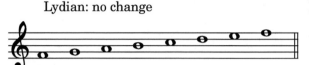

Mixolydian: major

Aeolian: harmonic minor

Ionian: already major

Aeolian: melodic minor ascending

Aeolian: melodic minor descending

The Mixolydian mode becomes a major scale (which is what the Ionian already is), the Dorian now corresponds to the melodic minor, ascending, the Aeolian is already the melodic minor in descent and, with *musica ficta*, becomes the harmonic minor. If the seventh degree of the Aeolian mode alone is raised, the distance between it and the sixth degree becomes a tone and a half, an interval not then regarded as 'singable'; this would be eradicated by raising the sixth degree also, a step that yields one more ascending melodic minor scale.

Another facet of *musica ficta* was the instinctive avoidance of an imperfect fifth either above *or* below the final, so that the fourth degree of the Lydian mode was habitually flattened, as in Ex. 14, producing another major scale.

Ex. 14

Lydian major

The implementation of these two types of change, both arising from what people thought *sounded* better, yielded three major scales (Ionian, and altered Lydian and Mixolydian) and a variety of minor scales, all of which are in common use in today's music. The Phrygian mode, perhaps the least used, did not attract these modifications – which would have led to a scale with both leading and leaning notes to the tonic (D♯ rising, and F falling to E). In the end this destroyed the modal system of individualistic scales, and opened the door to the concept of a smaller number of types, transposable to any tonic.

These changes took place gradually, over a long period, and represented 'gropings' toward an end that was not clearly envisaged by those concerned. Neither were they made consistently, least of all (one suspects) when they were confined to performance. Even at a later time it is often hard to be certain whether notes were meant to be affected in this way, since, however they were written on the score, the convention of their alteration was well known. In many cases the existence of a lute part has provided a valuable guide since tablature shows *where* the note was to be found and, therefore, its exact identity. In the absence of lute parts many such questions remain open.

The general 'rules' of *musica ficta* may be stated, but equally it is easy to find examples that contradict them, for the process was not applied consistently, nor was it time-restricted in that 'now it's not there, now it is'.

There were three ways in which *musica ficta* worked :
1. Horizontally, within one line or voice.
2. Vertically, applied to notes sounded simultaneously.
3. Diagonally, involving notes in successive chords but in a different voice in each.

The breakdown of the modal system was gradual. During a long period such changes were applied in particular situations rather than generally, so that one note might appear both inflected and unchanged in the same piece of music, according to context. Hand in hand with this went early signs of a sense of moving from one key centre to another, the underlining of transient tonics.

The following examples, showing these 'rules' at work, are all drawn from the works of one composer, Luis Milan:

i) The seventh degree of the Dorian, Mixolydian or Aeolian mode might be raised, especially at important points in the music, to give a semitone approach to the final (horizontal).

Ex. 15*a* (Milan)

Dorian mode, on base of A – A B C D E F♯ G A

The G in bar 1 *follows* the final and thus remains unchanged. That in bar 2, bass line, is not followed by an A and is also unaltered. In bar 3 the G does precede an A but, as may be confirmed by playing it with a G♯, would sound 'uncomfortable' if raised. The G in bar 4 leads positively to an A and celebrates it with a sharp.

ii) The fourth degree of the Lydian mode was lowered, to secure a perfect fifth above and below the final
(horizontal or vertical).

Ex.. 15*b* (Milan)

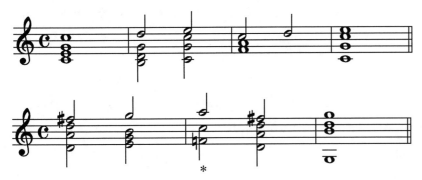

Lydian mode, on base of C – C D E F♯ G A B C

In the first quotation the fourth degree (F) is lowered to give a perfect fifth against the C in the upper part
of the chord and with the two Cs (bass line) on either side of it – both vertical and horizontal. In the second
it is lowered only in the third chord, to make vertical adjustment; the Fs in the upper line of bars 1 and 2
cause no offence and remain sharpened.

iii) Other notes might also be raised, to create a semitone approach to the next, higher degree, thus
gently 'underlining' it as a transient 'tonic', a centre of passing interest – one step beyond the use of only
the dominant for this purpose (horizontal).

Ex. 15*c* (Milan)

Phrygian mode, on a base of B – B C D E F♯ G A B

In the first extract the Ds are natural, i.e. normal to the mode. Those in the second are sharpened, establishing
the note E (fourth degree) as a temporary centre of interest. In modern terms we would say that the music
here reaches the key of E minor.

iv) When a note stepped up/down to the adjacent degree and then back again, the intervening note was often inflected to reduce the step to a semitone, thus smoothing the line (horizontal).

Ex. 15*d* (Milan)

Phrygian mode, on a base of D – D E♭ F G A B♭ C D

Lydian mode, on a base of F – F G A B C D E F

The first example shows the second and sixth degrees raised to produce semitone steps (bars 3 and 2 respectively).

The second quotation has the seventh degree (E) lowered in bar 2, but in neither of the other two bars, where it is not flanked by Ds.

v) The early Church abhorred, even feared, the tritone and called it *Diabolus in Musica* (the Devil in music) or the *quinta falsa* (false fifth).

Several procedures were followed in order to avert this fiendish intrusion into musical heaven:

a) When F and B were played together the F was raised or the B lowered, to avoid the (vertical) tritone.

Ex. 15*e* (Milan)

The B in bar 1 is lowered to avoid the tritone; the need does not arise in bar 2 and the B remains at the normal pitch for the mode.

b) A melodic line having the tritone notes as its highest and lowest points would be modified in the same way to avoid the embracing tritone (horizontal).

Ex. 15*f* (Milan)

The Bb in the final bar avoids the tritone between the highest and lowest notes of the bass line, the tritone drop from the previous bass note (in bar 4), and that within the final (shown) chord. The last note could have been harmonized with Bb in the bass, in which case the middle note would more likely have been a G.

c) These same two notes were similarly adjusted to avoid a tritone between the top note of a chord and the lowest of that following (diagonal). While this was an important factor in music for other media, in that for the lute and vihuela it did not seem to come into play. Ex. 16 shows two extracts that demonstrate the 'offence' itself and, at the same time, the composer's apparent unconcern. It is thought that, since the lute and vihuela lack sustaining power, the notes did not carry over sufficiently to be objectionable.

Ex. 16a (Crema)

Ex. 16b (Kargel)

Closely related to this is the matter of **false relations**. This 'crime' against the ear was committed if two notes of the same alphabet letter, but differently inflected, appeared in different voices and in quick succession. Ex. 17 gives two examples – which now sound little more than quaintly attractive, and again did not seem to greatly distress composers for the plucked strings. The second extract of Ex. 15b shows a false relation between the F♮ in the bass and the F♯ in the treble in bar 2.

Ex. 17a (Milan)

Ex. 17b (Dowland)

In Ex. 17a a B♮ in the bass line would have exposed a tritone with the preceding F – not in the top voice but prominent by virtue of its isolation; the false relation was clearly considered the lesser evil.

Musica ficta, so far exemplified only in art music, was not however confined to this area; it was equally applied in folk melody. The familiar 'Greensleeves' provides an interesting example. Many variants are in use and it is difficult to say exactly what the melody was in the beginning. In Ex. 18 enough of the tune is given to cover the areas of doubt; the remainder merely repeats the same situations.

Ex. 18

The note F at 1 varies from one version to another, as natural or sharp, but at 6 it is sharp in the lute version of Francis Cutting and, as there would be no real reason to make it so if it were properly natural in its mode, it is fairly safe to assume this to be its proper form, though *musica ficta* may have made it natural (sandwiched as it is between two Es). Likewise, the note G varies from G♯ to G through its many appearances, but at 5 Cutting gives it as a natural, and other versions invariably treat it in the same way; that at 2 is also natural in whatever version. G thus appears to be natural in its original form. This yields a scale of A B C D E F♯ G A – the Dorian mode. Indeed, any other view would lead to strongly improbable conclusions. The *musica ficta* process (iv) above would make the probable form of the F at 1 a natural and that at 6 a sharp. The G at 3 would originally be natural and there would be no reason to modify it, except perhaps in response to a later view of the accompanying harmony. At 4 the G is raised in approaching the A. At this point there are two Gs, though the 'need' to adjust to the following A exists for only the second one (cf. Milan: Fantasia I, Ex. 15a). However, it would be awkward and unvocal, at the required speed, to raise one G and not the other. Such a thing presented no problem in instrumental music and Mudarra makes *two* changes, in rapid succession, within one bar in Ex. 19. The first G♮ (normal in the mode) gives a semitone leaning note on to the F♯ that follows, the second G is raised to give a leading note to the A, while the third parallels the first and is, for good measure, flanked by two F♯s. The second quotation, from the same piece, shows Mudarra raising the G in approaching an A, with piquant effect.

Ex. 19 (Mudarra)

These changes came to support harmonic implications, that is, they were made with attention to their effect on the vertical sound of the music; primarily, however, their motivation was melodic. Nevertheless, when the underlining of temporary 'tonal' centres by semitones took root, the supremacy of the final, challenged – but never seriously – by the occasional focus on the dominant, perished. The way was open to the idea of one or two recurring scale patterns of proved durability (major and minor), moved from one level of pitch to another, to add variety. In short, the fate of the modal system was sealed. The process was accelerated by the rise of instrumental music *per se*, together with the growing emphasis on harmony and increasing awareness of the vertical effects produced, in passing, by lines of counterpoint. In speaking of 'major' and 'minor' scales we should remember that the descriptions apply equally to the modes themselves; our present major and minor scales *are* modes, and we still speak of C major and C minor as being the major and minor modes of C.

OTHER SCALES

There are, as we have seen, many possible kinds of diatonic scale, many not separately defined or discussed in textbooks; nor are they widely used. Any composer is free to devise his own variants and many have done so; the author bases the first movement of his *Prelude, Canto and Toccata,* Op. 38, on a 'non-standard' scale – C Db E F Gb A B C. Jazz music of the more traditional kind makes heavy use of a less clearly defined scale, sometimes referred to as the 'blues scale' or mode – C D E(b) F G(b) A B(b) C in which the melody varies in its choice of third, fifth or seventh degree (flat or natural) and sometimes moves, often by sliding, from one form to the other; the ambiguity (for that is what the choice amounts to) of the fifth degree came at a later stage. The scale is diatonic but some degrees receive variable inflection, and this provides one of its principal attractions. The scales used in Oriental music are extremely numerous and also depend on the inflections given to their different degrees, often less than a semitone.

No listing would be complete without the **chromatic scale** and **whole-tone scale**, the notation of which is arbitrary and dependent on context. These consist wholly of semitone and whole-tone steps respectively, and are therefore shapeless in that each note is equally distant from its neighbours, and none can, therefore, be clearly established by purely melodic means as a tonic, since this depends upon a scale with a distinctive pattern of tones and semitones. The chromatic scale serves as a sort of melodic 'lubricant', smoothing the way from one note to another at some distance of pitch, as in Ex. 20*a*, or providing a purposeful run-up to an important melody note (Ex. 20*b*).

Ex. 20*a* (Tárrega)

Ex. 20*b* (Tárrega)

The whole-tone scale, by its nature, contradicts any notion of an established tonic, and has been used by twentieth-century composers to create tonal uncertainty.

Melody

A melody is a succession of single notes, organized by some calculated or instinctive means. What is a beautiful melody to one person is 'tuneless' and incomprehensible to another. Ultimately, melody is in the ear of the listener, as is beauty in the eye of the beholder. It is possible to analyse and discuss melodies only up to a certain point, and many factors may be involved in their shaping.

SCALIC TENDENCIES

The degrees of a diatonic scale not only perform different functions within their tonal microcosm, they also have different levels of stability. If one plays Exs. 21a, b and c it is clear that the leading note, dominant and subdominant are not notes on which one could imagine allowing a melody finally to come to rest. One may pause on them, but only with the expectation of another, more restful note to follow. Nothing is as restful as the tonic, to which all these three notes will easily move directly, with a sense of finality. The term 'unstable' thus signifies that a note gives, in the context of the scale, some sense of incompleteness. In the last century we grew used to accepting almost *any* note at the end of a melody, provided that a convincing overall case is made out for it and, in judging stability, we must try to purge our ears of such universal tolerance and to listen simply.

When a note is unstable we say that it requires **resolution**; it must resolve on to another, more stable and conclusive, as though it poses a problem that must be resolved, or a pressure requiring relief. The same term will later be extended to intervals and chords and its meaning will be the same as here.

The resolution of the leading note on to the tonic is strong, the semitone step exerting a powerful pull. In similar fashion the subdominant may resolve downward on to the mediant (Ex. 21d) and, in the major mode, this too is a 'semitone step' and therefore compelling in its force.

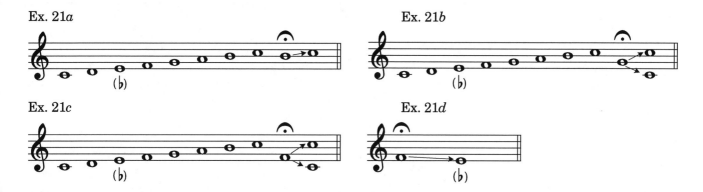

Even in the minor mode it works well because the mediant is a relatively stable note, even though melodies seldom end with it, and one step on either side of it leads to a more restless note – the subdominant (from which we have just moved) and the supertonic. The desire of the leading note to rise to the tonic and the subdominant to fall to the mediant will later be seen to have harmonic importance. If we regard each note of a major scale as being the tonic of its own scale, and append the number of signs in its key-signature, the result, for C major, will be:

C	D	E	F	G	A	B
(0)	(2♯)	(4♯)	(1♭)	(1♯)	(3♯)	(5♯)

The key of F may be described as the 'flattest' and that of B as the 'sharpest' of these signatures; the subdominant is termed the 'flattest note' and the leading note the 'sharpest'. The flattest note tends to fall and the sharpest to rise. In a major scale these are as above, but in others they may not be, for example in the harmonic minor scale –

C	D	E♭	F	G	A♭	B
(0)	(2♯)	(3♭)	(1♭)	(1♯)	(4♭)	(5♯)

The sharpest is still the leading note but the flattest is now the submediant; it remains true, though, that the flattest note tends to fall, this time to the dominant. Of course, if *any* note in *any* scale is one semitone removed from an adjacent degree it will tend to step up or down to it, whether it be the flattest or sharpest or not; thus, the mediant of the above minor scale still gravitates to the supertonic more strongly than to the sub-dominant – though it is happier not to move either way.

The dominant is highly unstable and, if we pause on it, the demand to resolve it seems irresistible and is best achieved by moving to the tonic, directly or by stepping along the scale to it, either up or down. The remaining degrees do not have sharply defined tendencies, though they are certainly unstable. In the major form both are separated from each of their neighbours by a whole tone and are thus, at face value, equally happy to move in either direction. The tonic will however pull more strongly on the supertonic, even in the minor form. Very restless notes flank the submediant (dominant and leading note), and each can lead equally directly to the tonic; in the minor form the tendency to fall to the dominant is the stronger. Exs. 21*e* and *f* illustrate these points and should be played and listened to:

Ex. 21*e*   Ex. 21*f*

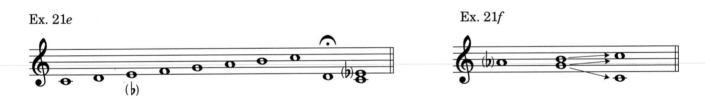

The above tendencies, at work in a variety of music, are shown in Ex. 22.

Ex. 22*a* (British National Anthem)

(Scarlatti)

Ex. 22*b* (Handel)

30

Ex. 22c (Sor)

Ex. 22d (Schubert)

Ex. 22e ('Good King Wenceslas')

Ex. 22f ('David of the white rock')

Ex. 22g (Beethoven)

Ex. 22h ('Good King Wenceslas')

a) First appearance of tonic on a weak beat hardly sounds like an ending; tonic finally emphasized from both above *and* below. Two examples given.

b) Subdominant falls to mediant (bar 2). Tonic finally established as in *a*, from both sides. Supertonic falls to tonic (bar 1) without feeling of finality.

c) Trading in both directions between tonic and leading note, and dominant and submediant. Note sharpening of D to give a leading-note effect to E.

d) Dominant rises, at end, directly to tonic.

e) Mediant steps down scale to tonic (bar 2). Submediant falls to dominant, which then steps along the scale to the tonic.

f) Minor mode: mediant gravitates to supertonic (bar 2) leaving feeling of incompleteness, preceded by step down from subdominant to mediant.

g) Supertonic rises to mediant, leaving a small 'question mark'.

h) Dominant steps down scale to tonic, then subdominant falls directly to tonic.

Examine as many melodies as patience allows, with a view to adding to the above examples.

These tendencies are strongest at the ends of melodies or at points within them where a positive approach is needed – ends of phrases, sentences, or sections. Elsewhere there is even more freedom and the guidelines are as often disregarded as followed. Most of the resolutions listed so far have been from one scale degree to the next (except for leaps from 4 or 5 to 1), but all leaps do not necessarily contradict natural tendencies. Leaps of a diatonic seventh amount to following a stepwise movement *in another octave*. In Ex. 23*a* the melody leaps twice by a seventh; in Ex. 23*b* these leaps are placed within a single octave and reduced to innocuous steps, the melodic line being denatured in the process:

Ex. 23*a* (Elgar)

Ex. 23*b* (bar 3 *et seq.* of *a*)

Ex. 24 shows several passages in which the guidelines are apparently ignored, but while we are dealing primarily with melody, the effect of harmony cannot be discounted. The two constantly interact on one another; melodic steps or leaps that do not conform to basic tendencies such as those discussed may be unremarkable in the context of the prevailing harmony. In Ex. 24*a* the leading note falls by a third instead of rising, in a minor key; Ex. 24*b* shows the same thing in the major mode. The supertonic rises twice in Ex. 24*c*, first by a third and then a fourth, instead of stepping up or down the scale. Similarly, instead of falling to the mediant, the subdominant falls (in *d*) to the supertonic; the leading note then rises by a third instead of moving to the tonic. Yet in none of these could the music be described as adventurous:

Ex. 24*a* (Frescobaldi)   Ex. 24*b* (Tórroba)

Ex. 24*c* (Ponce)

Ex. 24*d* (Sor)

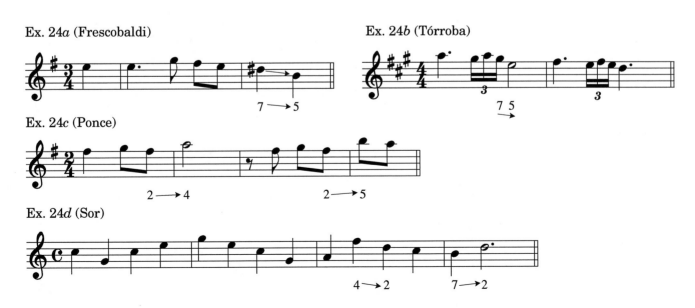

32

Chromatic alteration of a scale note automatically places it within one semitone of one of its neighbours and encourages it to gravitate in that direction; the alteration is often designed to bring this about. Thus in Ex. 25a the D♯ leads straight to the E; had it been a D♮ it might equally have pointed to C♯, as in Ex. 25b.

Ex. 25a (Castelnuovo-Tedesco)   Ex. 25b

Some chromatic inflections produce leaps through augmented or diminished intervals, though these can originate within the scale itself. Traditionally, after an augmented interval the melodic line moves outside the bounds of the interval itself (continuing in the same direction), while a diminished interval is followed by a move back to within the interval (reversal of direction). Exs. 26a, b and c show re-entry into a diminished interval; d and e step outside an augmented one:

Ex. 26a (Giuliani)

Ex. 26b (Handel)

Ex. 26c (Duarte)

Ex. 26d (Bach)

Ex. 26e (Duarte)

33

A composer may choose to ignore this trend if it suits his purpose. In Ex. 27b Ponce, thinking as much harmonically as melodically, first disregards it, then conforms in bar 2, and finally observes it in direction but does not step back *within* the interval. Bar 1 might be regarded as an octave displacement of the following note, the effect being much the same if the B is changed to that within the stave:

Ex. 27a (Rosetta)

Ex. 27b (Ponce)

One factor that often overrides the basic tendencies is that of scale movement *per se*, in passages whose flow carries them through in their own right and subjugates the individual 'whims' of at least some of the notes. Two such passages are shown in Ex. 28; there are countless others:

Ex. 28a (Sor)

Ex. 28b (Sanz)

Marked as these preferred directions of movement may be, they are frequently and easily reversed in practice either to give *increased* tension, since the 'natural' movements decrease it, or when some other factor, for example an extended scale passage, takes over.

CHANGING NOTES AND SEQUENCES

One of the means by which composers can make a melodic line more interesting is by the use of changing notes (*note cambiate*), as in Exs. 29*a* and *b*:

Ex. 29*a* (Dowland)

Ex. 29*b* (*ibid*)

Two appearances of a note are separated by one each of the two notes lying immediately above and below, in either order; as in the beginning of Ex. 28*a* the changing notes themselves may be chromatically altered for smoothness. This little group of four notes, obviously related to the *gruppetto* or turn, begins and ends with the same note and may thus be looked upon as a decorated version of that note, a more interesting way of presenting it. Note that the asterisked notes in Ex. 29*b* also produce a subsidiary, descending-scale effect. Though not strictly 'changing notes', groups such as those in Exs. 29*c-f* have the same effect:

Ex. 29*c* (Sor)

Ex. 29*d* (Anon.)

Ex. 29*e* (Dowland)

Ex. 29*f* (French traditional)

The basic group of Ex. 29d is immediately repeated one step lower, while those in Exs. b and e make two progressive downward moves. Such repetition is termed a **sequence**, and the basic unit is said to be developed sequentially. The overall effect of those of b and e is of a decorated, descending scale; that of d is like a normal changing-note grouping (F♯ G E F♯). The process is not restricted to short units such as the above but may involve larger spans, as in Ex. 30:

Ex. 30a (Farnaby)

Ex. 30b (Ponce)

Ex. 30c (Ponce)

Ex. 30d (Bach)

Ex. 30e (Rameau)

Ex. 30f (Sor)

Ex. 30g (Traditional hornpipe)

Ex. 30*h* (Bach)

Ex. 30*i* (Giuliani)

(*a*) A chain of five units plus one of a different type; (*b*) One simple step down with a four-bar unit; (*c*) A series of three units plus one that is irregular and incomplete; (*d*) One step down with a two-bar unit, the upbeat notes being varied; (*e*) A one-bar unit steps *up* once; far less common than a descending sequence; (*f*) As for (*e*) but with a two-bar unit; (*g*) A succession of four half-bar units, the step to the last one not matching the previous ones; (*h*) and (*i*) The unit is chromatically altered on repetition, indicating a temporary change of key. The unit in (*h*) is of two bars, in (*i*) of three plus one beat.

MOTIFS

The tendencies of notes to resolve in certain ways help to give impetus to a melody, changing notes and the like decorate it, and sequences assist in extending it. However, for the construction of a coherent whole, some binding material is invaluable. The simplest is that of the motif, a recurring and recognizable unit that may be rhythmic, melodic or both. The folk tune in Ex. 31*a* has a four-note 'cell' (D C A F) that recurs in different situations and rhythmic forms:

Ex. 31*a* (English traditional)

In *b* the rhythmic unit is easily identified and pervades the whole piece:

Ex. 31*b* (De Visée)

The unit in *c*, rise and fall with the top note repeated, is simple and effective:

Ex. 31*c* (Haydn)

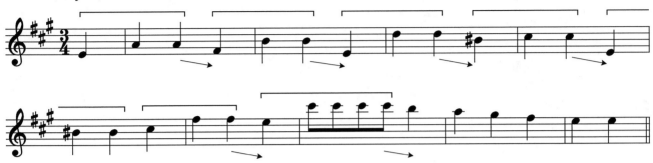

The rhythmic pattern of the first bar is used persistently in *d*:

Ex. 31*d* (Ponce)

Ex. 31*e* is unified by the basic cell (both melodic and rhythmic in shape) at A, and its inverted form at B:

Ex. 31*e* (Duarte)

Another common device is that of beginning and/or ending the sections or periods of a piece in similar fashion. Ex. 32 gives examples of beginnings. Ex. 32*a* faithfully reproduces the rhythm but follows the melodic pattern in outline rather than by precisely matching its intervals:

Ex. 32*a* (Scarlatti)

Both *b* and *c*, however, contain exact echoes – in *b* in the dominant key, in *c* in the relative major:

Ex. 32*b* (Bach)

Ex. 32*c* (De Visée)

The rhythm of the opening is precisely mirrored in *d* but the melodic line is inverted:

Ex. 32*d* (Haydn)

Endings are shown in Ex. 33. In *a* and *b* the section endings are exactly matched:

Ex. 33*a* (Weiss)

Ex. 33*b* (L. Couperin)

In *c* the melodic profile is modified to fit closure on to the tonic instead of the dominant:

Ex. 33*c* (Sor)

Three 'rhyming' endings within one piece are shown in Ex. 33d:

Ex. 33d (Bach)

The ending of *e* is of a type common in renaissance music, appearing in various forms. Composers tended to use one form more or less consistently within one piece; that of *e* recurs often.

Ex. 33e (Kargel)

On the largest scale unity can be achieved in terms of the total form or structure of a melody, but that is a more complex question.

STEPS AND LEAPS

Melodies can move by stepping from one scale note to the next or by leaping to one further removed (an interval not less than a third), termed **conjunct** and **disjunct** motion respectively. Conjunct motion includes movement from one chromatic form of a note to another, for example from C to C♯. Good melody balances the two to achieve variety; a tune consisting solely of leaps or steps would be boring. Composers of early music avoided the leap of a tritone, but today even this does not disturb us; there are now no 'forbidden' leaps.

Examples showing the balancing of conjunct and disjunct motion are shown in Ex. 34 – for brevity, now referred to as CM and DM. The line above the staff is straight during conjunct and kinked during disjunct motion.

a) The first phrase begins with extended CM whose flow is interrupted only near its end by DM. In the second DM is followed by CM which, with two small repetitions (asterisked), is even gentler than the first time. There is thus contrast within each of the two sections and between the two – CM/DM/CM versus DM/CM.

Ex. 34a (Traditional)

b) The relationship between the first and last four bars is clear, each having a DM/CM/DM/CM structure. The second has CM in only its first four bars, and CM/DM/CM in the final four. The four-note group immediately before the end contains one small leap (D to F), but this does not affect the impression of downward scale motion in that bar; if either *b2* or *b3* is substituted for this group the effect will be felt to be similar. It is in fact an example of *nota cambiata* (p. 35).

Ex. 34*b* (Dowland)

c) Again there is an obvious resemblance between the first and second four bars, each having a CM/DM/CM form. The last four share this structure but the balance is quite different, the DM entering much earlier. The second A in bar 5 is subsidiary and does not change the feeling of CM; if it is omitted and a crotchet (quarter-note) C played instead, little difference will be felt. Likewise, the C in bar 10 gives a little push to the last phrase, but its replacement by another D or E♭, or even a higher F, would not disturb things much.

Ex. 34*c* (Dowland)

41

d) The first example is an early sketch by Beethoven for the theme of the second movement of his Fifth Symphony; the second has the theme in the form he finally adopted. The first shows, apart from the re-start in bar 2, unrelieved CM, whereas the process of refinement leading to the final form included the introduction of DM, giving strength and variety.

Ex. 34*d* (Beethoven)

CADENCES AND CLIMAXES

In melodic use the degrees of a diatonic scale have different degrees of stability (p. 29) and, in this sense, all chromatic notes are obviously unstable. In the course of a melody use is made of these tendencies in finding points of tension or repose, but their effect depends on other factors also. The note D in Ex. 35*a* has tension, whereas those in *b* are unaccented and rub past too quickly to be more than a passing 'lubricant'. These tensions are implicit in the notes, within the context of a key, but are not solely responsible for shaping melody.

Ex. 35*a*   Ex. 35*b*

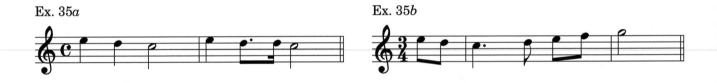

A literary story may be subdivided into chapters, paragraphs, sentences and phrases; music may be similarly analysed, the story being the work as a whole. If we take a simple melody such as Ex. 36 we can see that its opening statement divides into two short phrases and that these 'mirror' the words. The first says 'When three hens go into the fields...', provoking the question 'What then?', to which the second phrase replies 'the first one goes in front...' – like question and answer, balancing one another. At the halfway stage the note G, the dominant, is unstable and sounds unresolved, like the question itself; at the end, the question answered, the tune rests on the tonic. If we speak the words our voices inflect these points, falling a little in pitch at the end, and perhaps rising at the halfway point. Such places are called **cadences** (from the Latin *cadere*, to fall) whether in speech or in music.

Ex. 36*a* (French traditional)

Extending the literary parallel, a cadence giving a sense of finality or repose is equivalent to a full stop and is called a **full close**; when it does not it is comparable with a comma or semicolon – a **half close**. The tune in Ex. 36 has closes of both kinds, implied by the melody notes themselves – restless dominant, stable tonic – but the effect may be intensified by adding harmony, whether skeletal (as in *b*) or full (as in *c*). This does not *create* the cadence points but it does underline them.

Ex. 36*b*

Ex. 36*c*

This simple concept is not confined to nursery tunes but extends to larger areas; Ex. 37 shows eight-bar sentences ending on dominant and tonic in turn.

Ex. 37 (Sor)

On a still larger scale, many dance and other movements by (for example) Bach, Handel, Rameau, Haydn and Mozart, are in two sections (each usually repeated) of which the first ends on the dominant note and/or with dominant harmony, the second on and supported by that of the tonic. Section-endings from a few pieces having this kind of structure (termed **binary form**) are given in Ex. 38. The scheme is not found in *all* such pieces; in some, both sections may come to rest on the tonic, while the first section often 'half-closes' in the relative major key when the home key is minor. When used in this more spacious way, the process relates to the ground-plan or *form* of the music – a separate subject in itself. The famous musicologist Sir Donald Francis Tovey once wrote 'Form is melody writ large'.

Ex. 38*a* (Scarlatti)

Ex. 38*b* (Bach)

Ex. 38*c* (Mozart)

MELODIC CURVES

Many stories work their way to climaxes – some to moments of great tension, some to smaller crises, others to a series of climaxes of mounting intensity. Many simple narratives make their point gently, without need for strong climactic points. The same is true of tunes. A melodic climax is often associated with the highest note – either in its own vicinity or in the tune as a whole – pitch and tension tending to rise together, whatever the degree of the scale concerned. The melody of Ex. 36 rises to a peak at A, which equally emphasizes the G that follows, then subsides gently to the tonic to form a single, rising and falling curve. Within the section shown in Ex. 39*a* Sor's tune does likewise, the F♯ emphasizing its peak at the G.

Ex. 39*a* (Sor)

Ex. 39*b* (continuation)

Bars 1-8 repeated

In the continuation *b*, it first rises to a new peak. A, similarly underlined with a G, and then, having restated the opening section, mounts to its highest point, C, driven home by the acciaccatura D, and then descends steadily to its end. Its overall form is thus one of a series of peaks of ascending pitch. This same 'rising-wave' contour is also followed by music as diverse as the first section of the First Prelude of Villa-Lobos (the melody reaches up to D, then E, and finally to F♯), *La Arrulladora* (from Castelnuovo-Tedesco's *Platero y Yo*), the 'Londonderry Air', and Ex. 12*g*.

Melodies do in fact follow many kinds of curve, + and some other types are illustrated in Ex. 40:

Ex. 40*a* (Tárrega)

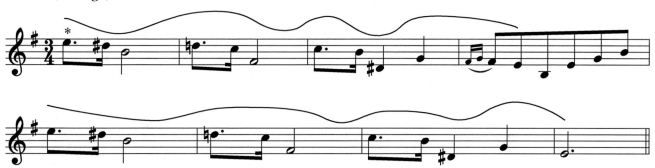

Each half has the same 'falling-wave' form, the two being joined by a re-ascent, like a ride on a scenic railway.

Ex. 40*b* (Traditional)

Three plateaux (the notes B, A and B) form a very flat 'curve', with the A as its trough, and are separated by deeper curves; after the peak there is a linear descent.

Ex. 40*c* (Duarte)

+ See *Harmony and Melody*, Book I, by Elie Siegmeister (Wadsworth). The examples are directly playable on the guitar.

A series of curves appears, peaking in the middle, like a serrated arch.

Ex. 40*d* (Duarte)

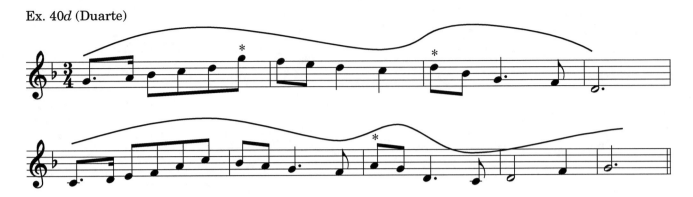

A succession of curves whose peaks (G, D, C, A) gradually descend (cf. Ex. 40*a*) but the line finally rises to G, completing an overall descent through an octave, G to G.

Ex. 40*e* (Schubert)

Curve and climax serve a dramatic purpose: in this example (Schubert's 'Death and the Maiden') the melody first follows a serrated curve, with F♮ at its peak, as the girl pleads with Death to spare her; Death then speaks in a calm, soothing but relentless voice (flat melodic line) the ebb and flow of tension being created by the harmony (not shown). In this second section the melody falls to an 'un-final' B at the halfway, then rises to the finality of the tonic (the inevitability of death) at its end. The harmony underlines the difference.

Some melodies seem to be anchored to or 'hypnotized' by a single note, to which they insistently return – like a piece of elastic, pulled out to different extents only to return to its relaxed one when allowed to. This type of melody seems to be characteristic of certain writers and is not common in the work of all. Examples would be Ex. 31*d*, when seen in the work's entirety, the same composer's Valse (Ex. 12*e*), and various pieces by César Franck, for instance No. 4 of the items arranged by Segovia (Schott GA 118) and the first and second movements of his Symphony in D minor. The opening melody of the second movement of Rodrigo's *Concierto de Aranjuez* similarly 'harps' on its dominant.

In summary: the notes of a scale have different degrees of repose or tension (*all* chromatic notes are unstable by nature) which help to control the flow of a melody and to establish cadence points. The rise and fall of a melodic line creates curves of many types, with peaks and troughs; the former tend to be associated with climaxes, whether associated with cadence points or not. The total shape of a melody is governed by its form or plan, a subject beyond the scope of this book.

Intervals

So far intervals have been treated only as measures of the rise and fall of a melodic line, but they have another equally important facet. When we play two different notes in succession we hear them as a brief melodic incident. When we play them simultaneously the sound acquires an identity of its own; the previously separate experiences fuse into a new and different one, the *harmonic* effect of the interval between them. By listening carefully and focusing our attention, we can distinguish the two notes, but the predominant impression is that of the character of the interval as such, and its emotional impact. When we play two notes together we have a **chord**, albeit an incomplete one, and we are already in the presence of harmony.

The placing of one note above another produces an interval or, better, a rudimentary chord; when one interval is piled on top of another, a complete chord may be produced and, if the process is repeated, extended harmonies result. To understand harmony we must first come to terms with intervals. For this, aural training is essential, and is something one *must* do for oneself. There are a few concepts that can help to ease the task. Intervals may usefully be classified by the impression they make on the listener. If we play the intervals of one of the following groups we may hear their 'family resemblances'; these may suggest different terms to different people, and those given are only the author's impressions of their emotional effects. The reader should compile his or her own lists, and will find them useful as a first 'sieve' when learning to identify intervals by their sound alone.

1. All perfect intervals: empty, strong, stark, severe.
2. Major and minor thirds and sixths: smooth, friendly, soothing, pleasant.
3. Major and minor seconds and sevenths: acrid, aggressive, disturbing, nasty.
4. The tritone: vague, unsure, lost, undecided, restless.

This listing does not include every interval that exists on paper – there are others, augmented and diminished – but it covers every possible distance from 0 to 12 semitones. The ear does not distinguish between enharmonic forms such as the augmented second and the minor third when they are played on an equal-tempered instrument (see p. 8) such as the guitar. The musical context usually makes clear which one is intended, but this is a question of 'grammar' rather than the aural effect of an isolated interval. Our present concern is with single intervals, which are first judged without reference to context; under these conditions it is natural for the ear to identify them as their simpler selves, for example a minor sixth rather than an augmented fifth.

In their harmonic use it is usual to divide intervals into two groups: **consonant** and **dissonant**, according to whether or not they seem stable and satisfying in themselves. This classification is open to personal judgement and to variation over the centuries but, in general, it may be taken as a reliable guide to traditional usage. The consonant intervals are those of groups 1 and 2 above, though the perfect intervals are sometimes termed 'perfect consonances' and the thirds and sixths 'imperfect consonances'; the perfect fourth is also termed 'dissonant' either when it is alone or when it is the lowest interval in a chord. The dissonant intervals are those of groups 3 and 4.

The simple fact is that there are no absolutes in musical usage and our views of what is good or bad, acceptable or intolerable, have changed constantly over the centuries. The earliest music made almost exclusive use of 'perfect' intervals, taking in those of group 2 at a fairly early stage. Since then, the history of music has been a chronicle of increasing tolerance, with each age accepting what the previous one rejected. Now we seem to have reached a limit and will accept virtually *any* dissonance for which a reasonable case is made out. Our progress through the remainder of the book follows, broadly speaking, a line through musical history, from the simple to the complex.

An important way in which intervals differ is in their strength. We define the strength of an interval as its sharpness of identity and assertiveness, on which basis the octave and unison are clearly the strongest of all. The exact tuning of two notes to give either of these should not tax any musical person. They correspond also to the lowest steps of the overtone series (p. 6), with frequency ratios of 1:1 (unison) and 1:2 (octave). In general, the lower down an interval may be found in the overtone series, the stronger it is – with its notes in natural, acoustic order – and, therefore, the next strongest interval is the perfect fifth (see Ex. 41*a*), with a frequency ratio of 2:3, almost as sharply focused as the octave.

Ex. 41

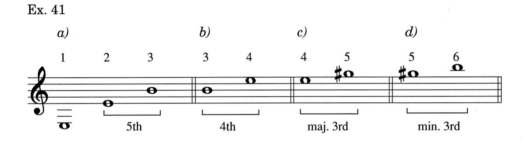

A violinist does not tune their instrument by taking each string individually; instead one draws the bow across pairs of adjacent strings and adjusts until one hears a perfect fifth. The guitarist who attempts to tune their instrument by seeking perfect fourths between pairs of strings (except for the 2nd and 3rd) is on shaky ground, for the interval is not strong enough for the purpose – it appears higher in the series (Ex. 41*b*). Instead, one is safer in relying on unisons and/or octaves. The same criterion shows the major third as a stronger interval than the minor, for which see *c* and *d*. The basic explanation of all this is complex and beyond the scope of this book; the interested reader is referred to Paul Hindemith's work *The Craft of Musical Composition* (Schott).

The Beginnings of Harmony – Triads

There is insufficient surviving evidence for us to know the exact nature of the earliest music, a field in which there is less than complete agreement among experts, but it is reasonably sure that melody preceded harmony (as we now understand it) by a very long time. The earliest Christian hymns and chants were melodic lines sung in unison and octaves (known as **magadizing**), taking in the second overtone. By the ninth century A.D. there had developed a practice known as **organum** which, in its severest form, consisted in singing each note of the melody together with another, a perfect fourth or fifth above it, so that they formed parallel lines, or even with *two* added lines moving in parallel octaves 'sandwiching' the original lines – see Ex. 42.

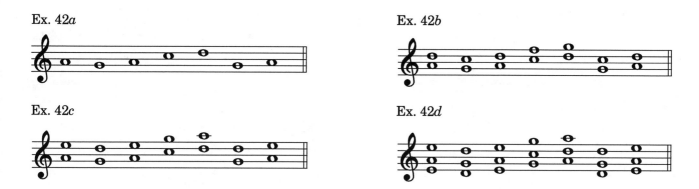

In freer organum the parts did not follow one another slavishly, at a constant interval, and had independence; but even here, despite the simultaneous sounding of two or more notes, the thinking was not harmonic in our present-day sense but, rather, the embellishing of the original melody and the emphasizing of important notes – as defined by the text of the hymn or chant.

At first it was felt necessary to eliminate the less 'pure' sound of the fifth from the end of a piece, finishing only with unison or octave, but eventually the fifth was admitted – progress to the third overtone. The use of thirds began at a very early stage, with free organum in fact, but they were regarded as dissonant and not accepted as consonant until much later. When they were, one more step had been taken up the overtone ladder.

TRIADS

While horizontal music (melody) was paving the way for vertical (harmony) it was already instinctively realized that the perfect fifth provided a stable framework. Such a structure lacks, however, warmth and comfort – though the simile is perhaps unkind to its strength and purity. Since mankind has always welcomed anything that helps to make a strong and severe regime a more pleasant place for sybarites, it was natural that the friendlier thirds should, once they infiltrated the system, be found to soften the effect of the perfect fifth, even though marring its purity. Musical mathematics being what they are, a perfect fifth may be divided into two thirds, in two ways:

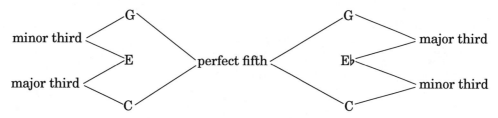

These resulting three-note chords are called triads (a name for *all* chords consisting of two thirds added together) and they are more precisely known as **common chords** – because they are the most ubiquitous chords in all music; and they are further described by the nature of the lower of their two thirds. Thus, C E G is a **major triad** (or common chord) and C E♭ G is a **minor triad**. In each case the third softens the starkness of the fifth in a way we still find agreeable. Both forms were, naturally, in use in early music, but were not given equal status.

The major triad exists in Nature, as the lowest six members of the overtone series, and has strength and comparative purity (now slightly sullied by equal temperament, which shifts the position of two of its notes) so that, when it was eventually found acceptable support to the last note of a piece, the major was admitted before the minor, the latter being felt too impure to act as a final concord (Narvaez' *Canción del Emperador* is a notable exception). Thus, both Luis Milan and Francesco Canova da Milano frequently ended their pieces with a chord that lacked its third when the mode was minor (Exs. 43*a* and 44*a*) or even without the fifth (Ex. 43*c*); occasionally they omitted the third even when the mode was major (Exs. 43*d* and 44*b*), though, in major modes, they did not hesitate to include it at other times (Exs. 43*b* and 44*c*). Among a total of over 150 works by these two composers, there is not one work in a minor mode that ends with a minor triad.

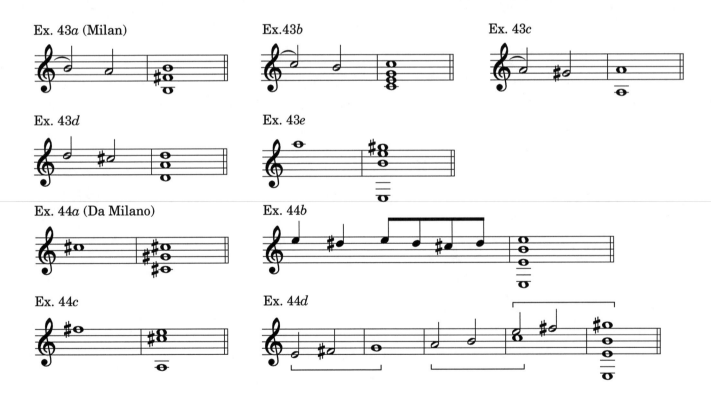

Ex. 43*a* (Milan)   Ex.43*b*   Ex. 43*c*

Ex. 43*d*   Ex. 43*e*

Ex. 44*a* (Da Milano)   Ex. 44*b*

Ex. 44*c*   Ex. 44*d*

A device much used in the Renaissance was that of placing a major triad at the end of a piece in a minor mode, known as a **tierce de Picardie** (a Picardy third). This too is to be found in the music of both the above composers – Exs. 43*e* and 44*d*; in the second, voices moving upwards emphasize the effect of minor turning to major. The *tierce de Picardie* has been with us ever since that time, for the beauty of its effect, a sense of lightness after darkness. Dowland used it frequently, even in ending some of his most doleful works – *Forlorn Hope Fancy, Semper Dowland, Semper Dolens,* and *Farewell*. Bach also used it often, though never with greater emotional effect than in ending the second *Kyrie Eleison* of his *B minor Mass*.

The effect of the common chord is to 'extend' the sound of the note on which it is based; it seems to give weight and depth to it. It appears in many situations, for it is the most important harmony of all, but it is at the final return 'home' that its effect is most powerful, where the return of the tonic with the final note is to be emphasized.

INVERSIONS

The notes of a triad are described as the **root**, third and fifth, the first being the note from which the whole springs (chords, like plants, grow from their roots), and we describe C E G and C E♭ G as 'C major' and 'C minor' triads respectively. An alternative, perhaps empirical, way of arriving at them is to take the first, third and fifth degrees of the major or minor scale whose tonic is the root of the chord we want:

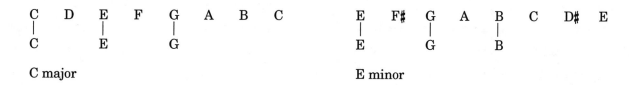

In this context they are not only common chords, they are also the **tonic chords**, a term that describes both their nature and function.

Before going further we should learn a little more about the common chords:

1. In the form in which we have derived them, either by splitting a perfect fifth or by building from the parent scale, their lowest note is the root, and we say they are in **root position**. It is clear, from even small experience, that either of the other two notes may on occasion be the lowest of all. When this is so, the chord is said to be **inverted**. If the lowest note is the third, we have a **first inversion** and, if it is the fifth, a **second inversion**. A triad is, like an interval, inverted simply by raising its lowest note by an octave:

Ex. 45

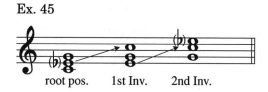

2. Triads may be used in incomplete forms. If we omit the root the residue is ambiguous, though the context may imply the identity: in Ex. 46 (where the root is given) the asterisked chord would be hard to hear as anything but C major.

Ex. 46

51

The third tells us whether a triad is major or minor and is known as the **characteristic note** of the chord, without which the chord is not fully identifiable. In early music the third was often omitted, especially at cadence points (Exs. 43*a*, d, 44*a*, *b*) where the strength of the remainder can be enough to replace a full major triad, and the neutrality effective in avoiding a minor (p. 55). The fifth is usually the best note to omit, the root and third being enough to convey the impression of the whole triad:

Ex. 47

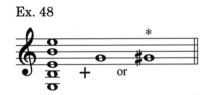

3. It is common for a triad to contain the same degree more than once (usually in different octaves) – and inevitable if the chord has four or more notes; this is termed **doubling**. Exs. 46 and 47 have the root doubled, even though the chords lack their third and fifth respectively; it is thus not essential that a chord be complete before a degree is doubled. The root is usually the best note to double, and the third the worst since its strong character tends to overbalance the whole sound. In playing Ex. 48 be careful not to strike any other note than the Bs and Es at first; then play the G or G♯ gently, and notice how this one quiet note can turn the whole sound towards major or minor.

Ex. 48

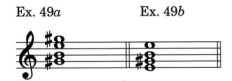

Heard in isolation, the chord in Ex. 49*a* sounds, with its doubled third, poor in character, especially when compared with *b* where the root is doubled. The third should never be doubled when it is the leading note of the prevailing scale. 'Rules' exist for guidance in doubling, but they tend to vary from one author to another and they may even go by the board when a chord is wanted primarily for its 'colouristic' effect. 'Does it *sound* right?' is always preferable to 'Does the *book* say it's right?'

Ex. 49*a*   Ex. 49*b*

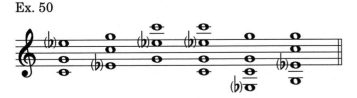

4. In Ex. 45 the notes of the chords are packed together as closely as possible and the chords are said to be in **close spacing** or distribution. They may however be used in more widely spread forms – **open spacing** (Ex. 50):

Ex. 50

52

or **mixed spacing**, with both close and open elements:

Ex. 51

With mixed spacings it is better not to have a close spacing between the two lowest notes; there is good theoretical reason for this, but the best reason of all is that it does not *sound* well. Careful comparison between the two chords in Ex. 52*a* will show this to the discerning ear, even though each has one third, one fifth, and the root doubled; the impact is less when the two chords are at a higher pitch, as in Ex. 52*b*.

Ex. 52*a*   Ex. 52*b*

Both types of distribution are common in guitar music, and where the third is immediately above the bass, the chord should not be played with too round a tone if it is to sound clear. Distributions with close bunching of notes in the lower parts and a well-detached treble part are equally hazardous. This is shown in Exs. 53*a* and *b*, the 'offence' again being smaller at higher pitch.

Ex. 53*a*   Ex. 53*b*

Closely packed sounds in the low register sound muddy – and the guitar is a low-pitched, virtually baritone, instrument. A simple demonstration of this can be made with a piano. Play a simple major triad, C E G, in the top octave of the keyboard, then repeat it in each lower octave in turn. As it moves below middle C it sounds increasingly muddy until, in the lowest octaves, it becomes a mere 'grumble'. The octave below middle C is the pitch of the lowest C E G playable on the guitar; guitar music is written an octave higher than it sounds.

5. No matter which note(s) may be omitted or doubled, or in what octave they appear, the lowest of all determines whether the chord is in root position – called a **direct triad** – or an inversion – **indirect triad**. Re-examine the chords in Ex. 46-53 and identify their positions (for answers see p. 158). The emotional effect of the three positions is markedly different. The root position has an air of repose and finality – play Ex. 54*a*, the final bars of the National Anthem, and note how much more satisfactory it is than *b* or *c*.

Ex. 54a   Ex. 54b   Ex. 54c

With *b*, the first inversion, there is a feeling of mildly restless consonance; *c* is unthinkable as a final chord and *demands* something else to follow it – like Ex. 54*d*. Even *b* sounds happier when completed as in Ex. 54*e*. We can describe the root position as fully stable, the first inversion as fairly stable, and the second inversion as aggressively unstable. This demonstrates, first, that the bass has a powerful influence on the overall effect; second, it shows that the influence depends on the identity of the bass note itself. Thus, the root position has, in the tonic chord (p. 51), the tonic of the scale as its foundation, a completely stable note. The first inversion has the mediant, a consonant but not fully stable note, and the second has the utterly unsettled dominant to sit on. The tendencies of the different scale degrees thus find a further expression, and melodic tendencies interact with harmonic ones; the two can seldom be realistically separated.

Ex. 54d   Ex. 54e

An example will illustrate the differences: In Exs. 55 and 56 the chords marked (1) are in root position and establish the key firmly at the start. Those marked (2) are first inversions and keep the music flowing gently, pushing it forward; had they been replaced by root-positioned forms the effect would have been stagnant, while second inversions would have sounded abrupt or even brutal. The chords at (3) seem to draw things to a head, preparing for the final return to the root-positioned final chords; their replacement by first-inversion chords would destroy that effect, and root-positioned ones would have weakened the impact of the final chords.

Ex. 55 (Sor)

Ex. 56

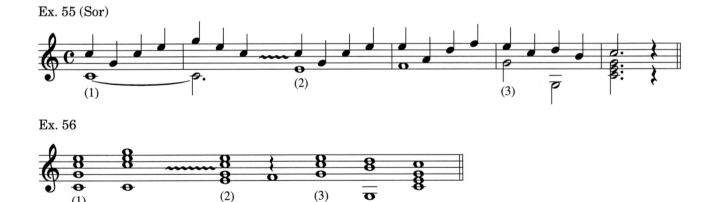

Examine as much simple music as possible (i) to identify the common chords, (ii) to determine their distribution and make-up (omissions and doublings), and (iii) to note their positions (direct or indirect) and to listen to the effect they make in the piece itself. Examples will be found that are expedient rather than musically inspired, of which Ex. 57*a* is typical; the short passage is effective, as shown, in establishing the key clearly but, at a later stage at least, it might have been enhanced by introducing a first inversion (as in *b*) – which would have increased the difficulty of an essentially simple study.

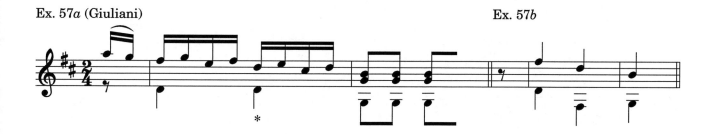

Ex. 57*a* (Giuliani)   Ex. 57*b*

7. The increasing tension associated with the progression from tonic-to-mediant-to-dominant, or with the use of root, third or fifth as the bass of a triad, has been discussed. It applies also to the top note of a chord; the highest and lowest notes are those which are exposed and, thus, most easily heard. A further 'league table' of stability can be drawn up:

top	R - 3rd - 5th	R - 3rd - 5th	R - 3rd - 5th
bottom	R	3	5

increasing instability

Most melodies end on the tonic, and when the supporting common chord is in its root position the maximum finality results. In contrast, a chord having the fifth as both highest and lowest notes is very unstable and challenging; such a chord was often used to set the stage for the cadenza in many classical-period concertos – back to the home key, but heralding dramatic events. Ex. 58, not from any particular concerto, is archetypal:

Ex. 58

allargando

Music should be examined from this viewpoint, the combined effect of bass and treble parts of chords. The forward propulsion of Exs. 55 and 56 owes something to this factor.

So far we have considered chords mainly as separate entities in their own right but have noted that melody and harmony cannot be treated separately, on the one hand, and on the other that triads seem to 'extend' the sound of the note on which they are based (p. 51). An isolated chord is no more or less significant than a single word in a dictionary; the ultimate absurdity is reached in 'chord encyclopedias' or '2567½ chords for the guitar' – as useful and musically significant as a catalogue of nuts and bolts in common use, or a dictionary of words whose use and meaning is not defined. A single chord is static, and the music cannot come to life until there is at least one change of harmony, giving a sense of progress. We have then to consider the composition of chords, their function in the music, and their relationship *to one another*.

If a triad 'extends' the sound of its root note, i.e. acts as a 'two-dimensional' form of that note, it is easy to appreciate that triads built on the degrees of one scale support the functions of the notes themselves. Thus, the concept of a tonic chord (p. 51) may be extended to other degrees of the scale, the most important of which are shown in Ex. 59, carrying their own triads:

Ex. 59

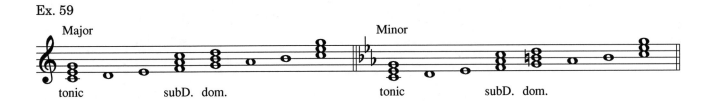

We now have the **dominant** and **subdominant** triads, as well as the tonic, and each one both emphasizes and 'colours' its root note. This states their *function* in that key, and develops naturally the principle of the transposition table (p. 13); just as the function of an individual note remains the same in all keys, so too does that of an individual chord. Thus, a chord of C major is tonic harmony in the key of C, dominant in the key of F, and subdominant in that of G; the function of a particular chord depends on the context of the key in which it finds itself.

SYMBOLIZATION

There are useful systems for abbreviation and shorthand of the written word; there are also those for indicating harmony. Of these, some aid academic understanding, others are strictly practical, for use by performing musicians. It is better at this point to define the bases of these systems rather than to follow them through in detail:

1. Functional symbols

These assist understanding but are not used in music intended for performance. Triads are symbolized by Roman numerals corresponding to their root notes; an upper-case number represents a major triad, a lowercase one a minor (or other, as yet unencountered, types of triad).

Ex. 60

Inversions are identified by subscript letters:

Ex. 61

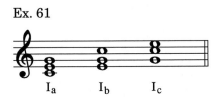

More complex chords add further symbols to the basic number.

2. Figured bass (thorough-bass)

This practical system was used in the baroque period by continuo players (early equivalents of the rhythm section of jazz or popular music) who were left to improvise and fill out accompaniments; it is still used by players of this kind of music but has no later extension. We shall pursue it, in this book, only to a limited extent, sufficient to give some impression of its basis; a full account is more properly reserved for a more specialized book.

The bass line of the music is notated in the bass clef, and numbers are shown below its notes; these indicate the intervals above the bass notes at which the other chord-notes appear. It is assumed that the intervals are diatonic in the home key, chromatic notes being shown by alterations to the numbers. By convention, the absence of any number below a note means that the chord is a root-positioned triad on that note, a '6' indicates a first inversion (short for 3.6), and '4.6' a second inversion, spoken of in reverse order (top to bottom!) 'six-four'. This is shown in Ex. 62.

Ex. 62

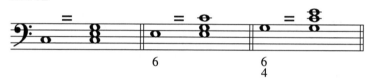

To avoid confusion, horizontal lines (lines of continuation) were used to indicate that a chord, or certain notes of one, persisted through a passage. Again, the symbolization of more complex chords entails the use of further numbers and other conventions similar to that above (no number above a diatonic, root-positioned chord).

3. Alfabeto

In this totally practical system, used in some early guitar tablatures, certain chord 'shapes', i.e. actual fingerings on the instrument, were shorthanded to alphabet letters. The letters had no relationship to the composition or function of the chords. Some knowledge of this system is important only to those concerned with that area of music.

4. Chord symbols

This is a practical shorthand system, developed for use in jazz and light music in the twentieth century. Symbols, which are not universally standardized even now, are used to describe a chord without reference to its function, inversion, makeup in terms of spacing, doublings or omissions. Major triads are described simply by the letter-name of their root note: thus C E G is symbolized as 'C', 'major' being understood, and represents a licence to use *any* form of that chord, governed only by convenience, good taste and imagination. Minor triads are similarly shown, with the addition of 'm', 'mi' or 'min' e.g. C Eb G = Cm, Cmi or Cmin. The symbol requires various extensions and the knowledge of certain conventions (like that of 'major' being understood) when used with more elaborate harmonies. Despite its obvious limitations and its non-functional character, the chord-symbol system has gained wide currency in practice and a knowledge of it is useful to most performing musicians today.

All chord-abbreviation systems have their use and value, though it may be highly specialized, as with figured bass and *alfabeto*, and all suffer from the same limitation. Every system starts from a simple basis – a simple numeral, few numbers (or even none), or single letters, but every extension or modification of the harmony requires a concomitant change in the symbol; there comes a point at which the symbol becomes at least as complex as the staff notation it is intended to obviate; under such circumstances it virtually loses its *raison d'être*. The widely used chord symbols have no means of showing omissions from chords, and some very simple combinations of notes, for example C G F, require symbols that are, in relation to what they purport to simplify, elaborate. *Alfabeto* was confined to a simple stock of chords and did not extend beyond them; it was not therefore subject to such a 'moment of truth'. Every system serves the immediate purpose for which it was devised, but does not extrapolate happily into more complex music.

Functional Harmony and Cadences

We have now established the notion of harmonic function, as distinct from the 'trivial' identity of particular chords in isolation, and have formed triads on the three most important degrees of major and minor scales – those in the minor are, properly, based on the 'harmonic' form of the scale. Interest now focuses on the connections between chords and the ways in which they may follow one another to form **progressions**.

1. Each note of a chord is to be considered as though sung by a voice or played on a single instrument; when the harmony changes each voice must move to its proper place in the next chord, a process known as **voice-leading**.

2. In the light of 1, the progress of each voice is to be regarded as melodic. In keyboard studies of harmony it is usual to assign a defined pitch-range to each voice, more or less corresponding with the registers of the human voice. The smaller range and technical problems of the guitar usually frustrate efforts to apply such clearly defined practices, and a freer attitude must be accepted.

3. Conjunct motion gives the smoothest melodic movement; this applies equally to the course of any one voice in a chord progression.

4. A corollary to 3 is that the movement of a voice by a semitone helps to make progress from one chord to another positive – the leading-note effect when rising, the leaning-note when falling.

5. Though not a stepwise movement, direct progress from dominant to tonic is a powerful melodic tendency which, when the roots of two chords stand in this relationship to one another, is transferred to the chords themselves, even though no one voice may actually move in that way. This corresponds with a natural 'with-the-tide' movement around the circle of keys, forward through the flats, since each tonic (root) becomes a dominant (root) at the next step (G to C, C to F etc.).

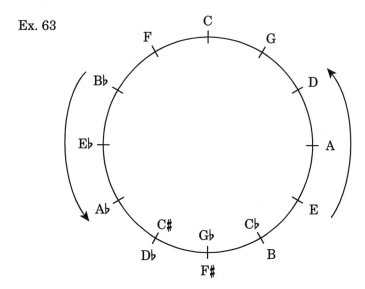

Ex. 63

6. Like people, chords enjoy firm relationships when they have something in common. The sharing of notes thus establishes a direct connection between chords – shared notes are called **common notes**.

We may now apply these considerations to the chords of the tonic, dominant and subdominant of a key; we shall use C as our example but the reader should work in other keys also. The possible connections between pairs of these chords may be shown as follows:

MAJOR

G══════G	A	G
D	E ──→ F	D
B ──→ C══════C ──→ B		
V	I	IV	V

MINOR

G══════G ──→ A♭ ──→ G
D ──→ E♭	F	D
B ──→ C══════C ──→ B
V	i	iv	V

As we are interested in the connections between the chords, they are placed in convenient order, not necessarily in root position. Common notes are shown (═══) and semitone steps marked (──→); there are also various whole-tone steps available, for example the D in the first chord (V major) can move either down to C (in I), or up to E.

These bonds are always available but, at this stage, we confine ourselves to the most important situations. Crucial stages in a piece of music, though often implied in a melodic line, are reinforced by harmony (p. 42); these are the cadences. The importance of a message lies in the words, but is even better conveyed if they are spoken in a suitable tone of voice. We now bring together the two concepts of cadence, and the chords based on the most important degrees of the scale, seeing how they may enhance one another.

There are two basic types of cadence: the **full close** or **perfect cadence**, which gives a sense of finality, and the **half close** or **imperfect cadence**, which does not.

PERFECT CADENCES

Referring to the above chart of connections, and points 4-6 on page 59, the authentic cadence is motivated by:

a) a common note (G) that, as dominant of the key, is highly unstable. This is most pronounced when it is the root of V, and subdued when it is 'demoted' to the fifth of the tonic chord.

b) a strong **root progression** (para. 5, p. 59), dominant to tonic.

c) a leading note that points to the tonic (B to C), plus a second one (D to E♭) in the minor form, underlining the mediant.

These three factors combine to make the authentic cadence strong and positive, like closing a door firmly. It is the most powerful of all ways of arriving at a musical conclusion.

The plagal cadence is activated by:

a) a common note (C) that is restful, the tonic of the key, anticipating the final note itself.

b) a smooth but 'permissive' rather than 'imperative' root progression (F to C) moving 'against the tide' of the key circle, which flows more firmly in the opposite direction.

c) a leaning note (F to E) that settles with a sigh of relief on to the mediant of the major key; in the minor it is A♭ to G, homing in on the dominant, the fifth of the tonic triad.

The plagal cadence is thus smooth but less powerful than the authentic, like closing a door gently. Its alternative name of **amen cadence** reflects its air of peaceful acceptance and its common use at the endings of hymns. Ex. 64 shows examples of authentic and plagal cadences:

Ex. 64 (Authentic)

(Plagal)

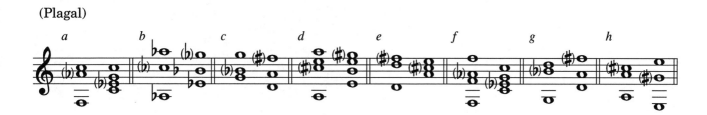

Authentic

i)   With only three parts, moving correctly, it is not possible for *both* chords to be complete; see (*a*), (*b*), (*d*) and (*e*).

ii) Though less satisfactory in effect it is not 'forbidden' for the leading note (third of V) to *fall* to the dominant, as in (*h*). With this concession both chords can be complete.

iii) In (*b*) both third and fifth of V move to the same note (D), leaving a bare octave. With three instruments or voices a unison would result, but with the solo guitar it is often reduced to one single note.

iv) The dominant note (root of V) can, in an upper voice, fall to the mediant, even though it is neither a root progression nor a conjunct movement; see (*g*).

Plagal

i)   Again, with the optimal movement of three parts there cannot be two complete chords, though (*g*) allows the tonic to rise gracefully to the mediant to bring it about.

ii) In the bass the subdominant note (root of IV) falls or rises directly to the tonic, (root of I); it may also do so in a higher voice even though it tends naturally to drop to the mediant, as in (*f*).

iii) The submediant (third of IV) can rise directly to the tonic, as in (*h*).

Strict part-writing is not always observed in guitar or lute music, voices appearing and disappearing freely, but in good writing the important elements in voice-leading, for example semitone connections, are respected.

Ex. 65 shows perfect cadences in guitar, lute and vihuela music:

Ex. 65

(i) (Authentic) *a* (Sor)   *b* (idem)   *c* (idem)   *d* (idem)   *e* (Giuliani)

f (idem)   *g (idem)*   *h (idem)*   *i (idem)*

j (idem)   *k* (Carulli)   *l* (Da Milano)

m (idem)   *n* (Milan)   *o (idem)*

p (Tansman)   *q (idem)*   *r* (Rodrigo)

Ex. 65 (ii)

(Plagal)   *a* (Narvaez)   *b* (Dowland)   *c* (Milan)   *d (idem)*

e (Da Milano)   *f (idem)*   *g (idem)*   *h (idem)*

i (Franck)   *j* (Ponce)   *k* (Tórroba)   *l* (Duarte)

1. Classical guitar composers were notably reluctant to use the plagal cadence; the examples are thus taken from the works of renaissance (lute and vihuela) composers and twentieth-century writers.

2. Composers of the last century seldom used such an unsophisticated device as a perfect cadence in its pure form, unless evoking an earlier style of music. Contemporary examples are thus few.

3. Notation in the classical period was often imprecise, sometimes showing a lingering influence of tablature (a system of notation showing when notes are played, but not how long they last). In performance therefore, the first E in bar 1 of *b* (authentic) would sustain for one beat and the G would persist into the final chord – which would thus be completed in four voices. Similar cumulative effects obtain in bar 1 of *g* and bar 2 of *k* (authentic).

4. The plagal cadences *b, d* and *h* end with a *tierce de Picardie*.

5. The examples show both observance and disregard of strict part-writing, and relate, variously, to the value placed on such matters in the period concerned (greatest in the Renaissance and Baroque), the weight of sound required in the final chord, and the quality of the writing – the intrusion of expedience as in *i* (authentic).

When, as in the above examples, both chords are in their root position, the result is described as a **direct cadence**. The first chord of a cadence may be inverted –

Ex. 66 (Authentic)   (Plagal)

and, less conclusively, the tonic chord may appear in its first inversion, which is regarded as consonant:

Ex. 67

When neither chord is in root position the cadence is **indirect**. This is not common, especially at important 'crisis' points, and is largely confined to two-part writing. Ex. 68 gives an example with a curious ending to *b* in which the tonic chord is deliberately, and perhaps needlessly, inverted. However, the connections between chords exist at *all* times, every cadence is not meant to be strong in effect, and chords may follow one another in the course of a phrase where no cadence is implied. Under such conditions chords may, if inverted, maintain a better flow. A special and important instance of an inverted cadence is given in the next section. As Exs. 66 and 67 show, it is possible, with an inverted cadence, to have two complete chords with only three voices.

Ex. 68*a* (Carcassi)   Ex. 68*b* (Giuliani)

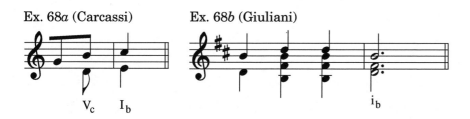

63

IMPERFECT CADENCES

I or i ⟶ V —— the half close

V ⟶ ? —— the deceptive, surprise, or interrupted cadence

The half close has the same connections between tonic and dominant; chords are the same as with the authentic cadence but (i) the root progression moves against and not with the tide, and (ii) the dominant note is 'upgraded' to a place of prominence as the root of V, stressing the unfinished character of this cadence. The two chords, taken in isolation, have the effect of a plagal cadence – the root falls by a fifth or rises by a fourth; the examples of Ex. 69 are thus given, preceded by the home scale in order to put them in context:

Ex. 69a

Ex. 69b

Ex. 69c

Ex. 69d

This emphasizes that chords *per se* are significant only when in a 'live' musical situation. A few examples from the repertoire are in Ex. 70 and require no comment; (*a*) and (*b*) are indirect, the others direct:

Ex. 70a (Carcassi)

b (Sor)

c (Giuliani)

d (Bach)

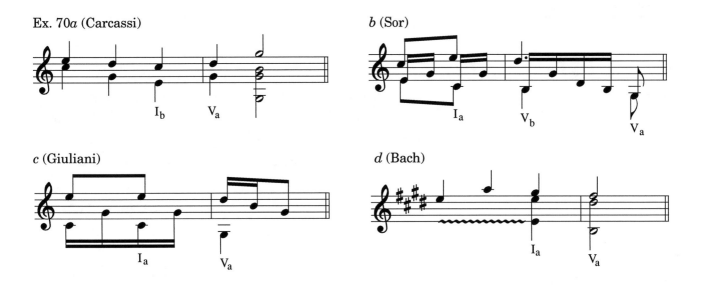

The common chord is unstable and challenging in its second inversion (p. 54) and is often referred to as a 'six-four' chord (p. 57) . The tonic six-four, with the dominant note as its bass, *demands* resolution and will lead very firmly to Va (6/4 resolves on to 5/3). When allowed to do so it is termed a **cadential six-four**. Six-four chords appear in pre-baroque music; their recognition and cadential use dates, however, from the Baroque. The six-four thus forms the basis of the most powerful form of half-close. A few examples appear in Ex. 71 – play the relevant scale before playing each of these. Again, the cumulative effect within a bar comes into play, i.e. some chords are arpeggiated:

Ex. 71a (Carulli)   Ex. 71b (Sor)

Ex. 71c (Giuliani)   Ex. 71d (Mozart)   Ex. 71e (Weiss)

The deceptive cadence can be only loosely defined. It occurs when, usually through the offices of the dominant chord or a six-four, the ear is led to expect a full close, but is met with an unexpected chord; this latter normally contains the anticipated tonic note, often as the melody note, but supported by 'foreign' harmony. The expected resolution often takes place soon afterwards, hence the term 'interrupted' (or sometimes 'delayed') cadence is applied. It is not necessary to discuss the nature of the substituted chord(s) at this point; merely playing and listening to the few examples in Ex. 72 will convey the impression of this type of cadence.

Ex. 72a (Haydn)   Ex. 72b (Bach)

Ex. 72c (Weiss)

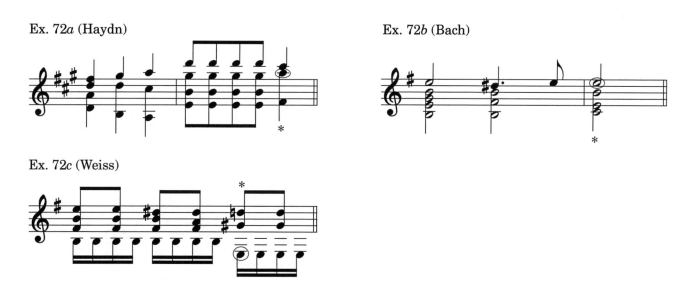

Primary Triads and Harmonization

The triads on the three principal notes of the scale (tonic, dominant, subdominant) are known as the **primary triads** of the key. These chords have served composers faithfully for centuries and without them much of today's popular music would vanish – their use by writers of humble ability has earned them the name of the 'three-chord trick'. The fact that they enhance the three main degrees of the scale is important but, equally, they contain among them every note in the major scale; the minor mode is less well defined, as is the minor scale itself. Below, the degrees of the major scale are set out, together with the primary triads that contain them:

1	2	3	4	5	6	7
I	V	I	IV	V	IV	V
IV				I		

Thus, in theory at least, any diatonic melody in a major key may be harmonized by using only primary triads. In fact it is not always acceptably so and results are sometimes dull and crude; it is however a starting point. The unclear identity of the minor scale (p. 15) creates problems at this level:

Harmonic form:	1	2	3	4	5	6	7
	i	V	i	iv	V	iv	V
	iv				i		

As with the major scale, there is at least one chord here for each degree, but the melodic form differs.

Melodic ascending:	1	2	3	4	5	6	7
	i	V	i	iv	V	–	V
	iv				i		

Melodic descending:	1	2	3	4	5	6	7
	i	V	i	iv	V	iv	–
	iv				i		

In each of these there is one degree that cannot be found among the primary triads derived from the harmonic minor scale. The problem may be solved, unsurprisingly, by using chords foreign to the harmonic scale, but, of course, native to the melodic forms. For instance, a major triad may be used in place of the 'proper' minor on the subdominant of the ascending melodic scale (Ex. 73), a process sometimes quaintly referred to as 'borrowing from the major' or, more evocatively, as the use of the **Dorian sixth**; the Dorian mode has a minor third and a major sixth. Conversely, the minor form of the subdominant chord is useable in the major mode to give a more 'pathetic' form of plagal cadence (Ex. 74) with two leaning notes.

Ex. 73 (Bach)

Ex. 74 (Ponce)

In both cases the 'foreign' chords are more properly describable as chromatic chords, as distinct from diatonic, for example the primary triads.

As a simple exercise, the primary triads are applied to the beginning of the National Anthem (Ex. 75a), treated as 'coloured blocks' of sound rather than as expressions of correct part-writing:

Ex. 75a

a) defines the key, the right choice for the first note.

b) IV is also possible but sounds unconvincing – try it.

c) d) e) When IV follows V the effect is often weak; I is the better choice in each case.

f) I brings the phrase to a full close, the obvious choice.

Though the above harmonization is not incorrect it is crude. The leaden effect of having every chord in root position can be alleviated by inverting some of them (Ex. 75b), but the result is still not really satisfactory:

Ex. 75b

With some tunes an acceptable solution *can* be provided by using the primaries alone, as in Ex. 76: the chords are direct in (a); some are inverted in (b).

Ex. 76a

Ex. 76b

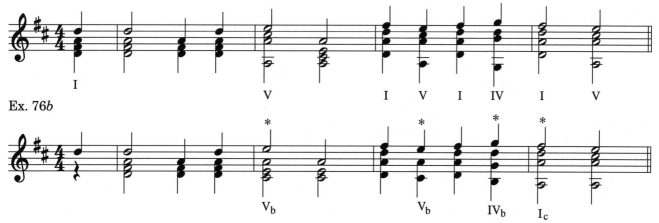

INDUCED HARMONY

A passage such as Ex. 77*a* sounds well, but if the notes are presented more quickly, either by reducing their length, as in *(b)* and *(c)*, or merely playing the music faster, it begins to sound over-busy. If played quickly enough it will sound irritating, like a kaleidoscope that presents a series of images too quickly to allow them to be seen properly before they vanish.

Ex. 77*a*   Ex. 77*b*   Ex. 77*c*

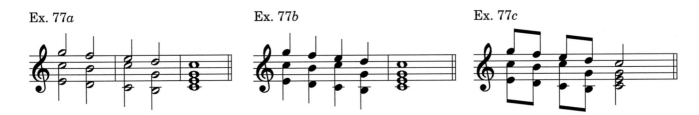

We do not need to attach a chord to *every* note of a melody, especially when it flows quickly. Any one note of a melody may belong to the harmony of the moment – or it may *not*. Those that do are called **essential notes**, those that do not are **unessential notes**. Sometimes the notes of a melody 'traverse' or arpeggiate the current harmony; they are then termed **byetones**:

Ex. 78

Unessential notes are classified according to the way in which they occur:

1. The **unaccented passing note** occurs in places where there is little emphasis, for example in the midst of a beat, as a mere 'lubricant', often completing an overall scale movement:

Ex. 79*a*

2. The **accented passing note** or **appoggiatura** falls on the beat, receiving an accent, as in:

Ex. 79*b*

3. The **auxiliary note** is sandwiched between two appearances of the same note and may be either above or below it, separated in most cases by no more than a whole tone.

Ex. 79c

4. The **suspension** occurs when an essential note is sustained while the supporting chord changes to one to which the note is unessential. The suspended note then steps up or down to conform to the new harmony:

Ex. 79d

If we reverse the process described above and decelerate a piece of music containing unessential notes in any form, especially 1–3, we become aware of the abrasive effect of these notes against chords to which they do not belong. The development of music over the centuries is however the growth of toleration; with time, therefore, the effect of the dissonance may become less offensive and found to be interesting in itself. The unessential note may become absorbed into the 'hostile' environment and a new chord born. Such a process has taken place repeatedly in musical history and represents a natural way of generating harmony, through a melodic process. The result is termed **induced harmony** – through the induction of fresh notes.
An important example of this mechanism is shown in Ex. 80:

Ex. 80   Ex. 81

At the asterisked points a chord is formed by adding the subdominant note to the dominant triad, and it is very important. Written in its close-spaced, root position (Ex. 81) it is seen to consist of the dominant triad with the minor seventh above: i.e. the root, third, fifth, and seventh. This chord is known as the **dominant seventh**, the first of several chords of the seventh we shall meet; it is also described as the **primary seventh** of the key. Various points should be noted:

1. Following the method of piling thirds together the dominant seventh results from adding a further diatonic third to the dominant triad.

2. The interval between the third and seventh is a tritone, the first really dissonant interval in any chord so far. The tritone is highly unstable and wants to resolve; this imparts 'motive power' to the whole chord, making onward movement compulsive – a new situation.

3. Like *any* four-note chord the dominant seventh has three inversions (Ex. 82*a*), of which the third is very unstable. Alternative distributions, easier to play on the guitar, are shown in Ex. 82*b*.

Ex. 82*a*   Ex. 82*b*

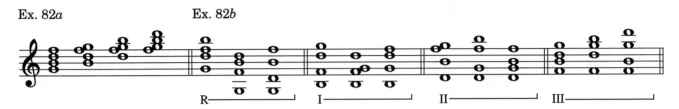

4. The tritone strongly tends to contract or to expand, according to whether it is a diminished fifth or an augmented fourth – which depends on the layout of the chord. Leading note and subdominant follow their natural melodic tendencies (p. 29), in rising and falling respectively.

Ex. 83

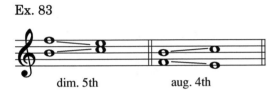

dim. 5th   aug. 4th

5. The movements of the notes in resolving the dominant seventh on to the tonic triad are (cf. p. 60):

The other connections (root-progression and whole-tone steps) remain as before. In the minor form the subdominant note (F in the above) is equidistant from mediant and dominant but still tends to fall to the former.

6. The extension of dominant harmony to the seventh adds a strong magnetic pull to the full close (Ex. 84*a*); the half close sounds even more unstable and difficult to pause on (Ex. 84*b*). Other examples of the full close are shown in Ex. 85.

Ex. 84*a*   Ex. 84*b*

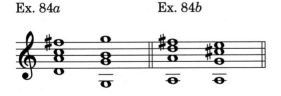

Ex. 85a (Sor)   Ex. 85b (Giuliani)

Ex. 85c (Aguado)   Ex. 85d (Ponce)   Ex. 85e (Ponce)

7. The seventh itself is now the characteristic note (without it only a triad remains) and is not to be doubled
    or omitted. The fifth is once more the best note to omit; see Exs. 85d and e.

8. When the tonic chord follows the dominant seventh it is not always in the nature of a cadence:

Ex. 86a (Beethoven)   Ex. 86b (L. Couperin)

Ex. 86c (Sor)   Ex. 86d (Legnani)

9. Only one tritone, between the third and seventh degrees, is available within a major scale; it thus defines
    the key and points to its tonic triad – each tritone is peculiar to one major key. Other tritones are possible
    in the minor mode (Ex. 87) but the orienting influence of that between the third and seventh degrees still
    overshadows that of the others.

Ex. 87

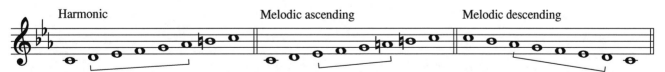

10. Symbolization

i) The functional symbol is V7, plus inversion lettering, e.g. V7c.

ii) The chord symbol is that of the basic major triad, plus '7' e.g. G B D/F = G7. The seventh is assumed, in the symbol, to be minor.

iii) The numberings are abbreviated as in Ex. 88. In the minor mode the third (leading note of the key) must be shown as being raised – the same is of course true of the dominant triad itself. In the first inversion this occurs automatically as the third is the staff-notated bass note.

Ex. 88

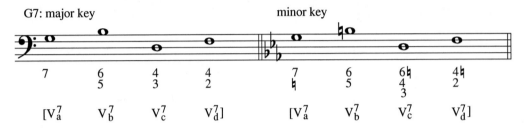

When the third is inflected the figure 3 is omitted, the accidental sign being understood to apply to the third.

EMBELLISHMENT OF THE FULL CLOSE

Cadences are often emphasized by decoration, just as we tend to embellish them with gestures when speaking. The process can be elaborate, but for the present only the simple methods, using diatonic (including passing) notes, are listed:

1. One of the commonest methods is the addition of a trill to the dominant chord (Ex. 89a). A trill may be open-ended or 'unfinished', as in the foregoing example, or it may be defined and 'finished' by means of changing notes, as in Ex. 89b. Although the trill in b is shown only as a trill sign in the original, its content is defined by contemporary convention; that in c is fully detailed in tablature. Trills are of course extensions of the auxiliary note (p. 69).

Ex. 89a (Bach)

Ex. 89b (L. Couperin)   (Dowland)

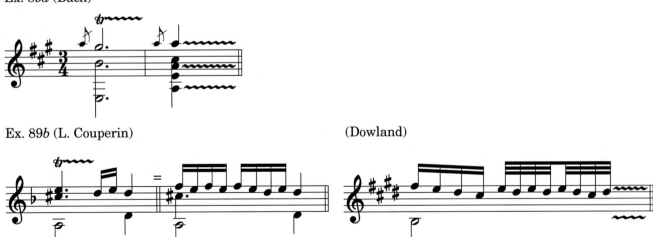

2. Decoration may consist of interposing adjoining or changing notes, as in Ex. 89c:

Ex. 89c (Collard)   (Mudarra)

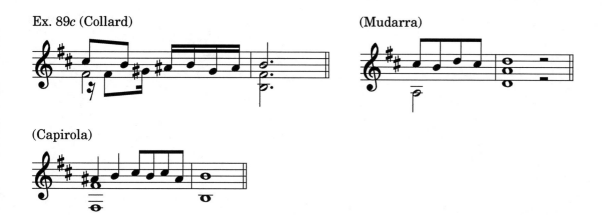

(Capirola)

3. Another common method is the suspension of the tonic note above the dominant chord (which accordingly lacks its third): see the last beat of Ex. 79b. The tonic note need not be suspended into the dominant chord but may simply be reiterated with it, as an appoggiatura. Examples are given in Ex. 89d.

Ex. 89d (Milan)   (Crema)

(Spinacino)   (Da Milano)

(Reusner)   (Cutting)

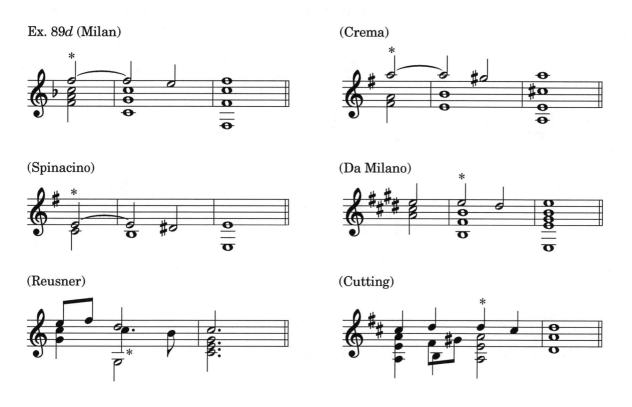

4. The tonic note may be introduced as an auxiliary:

Ex. 89*e* (Morlaye)   (Morley)

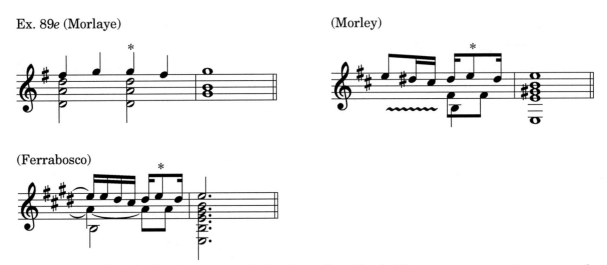

(Ferrabosco)

5. The seventh of the dominant seventh chord may be either held over as a suspension, or merely repeated to form a dissonance with the tonic chord (lacking its third) and finally resolved. This usually yields a **feminine cadence**, that is, one resolving on a weak beat of the bar, as distinct from a **masculine cadence**, which has the final tonic chord on the first beat – as with most of the cadences so far shown.

Ex. 89*f* (Sor)   (Traditional)

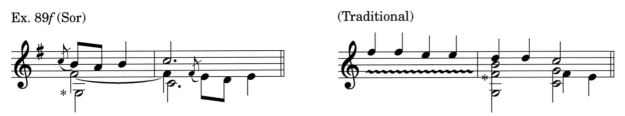

6. Conversely, the dominant seventh chord, usually incomplete, may appear as an **appoggiatura chord** above the tonic note, at a point where the plain tonic chord might have been expected – a sort of deceptive cadence, though not usually listed as such. As with (5) such cadences are usually feminine:

Ex. 89*g* (Carulli)   (Bach)

(Sor) (masculine)

Secondary Triads and Substitution

The primary triads stand on the three principal degrees of the scale; others may be erected on the remaining degrees and are termed **secondary triads**. Those in the major mode are shown in Ex. 90 and take the names of the degrees on which they are sited, for example mediant triad. That on the leading note consists of two minor thirds and is in consequence bounded by a diminished fifth (the primary triads have a perfect fifth), a new and dissonant type known as a **diminished triad**.

Ex. 90

ii   iii   vi   vii°

The diminished triad is symbolized as follows:

   i) The functional symbol, vii°, shows that the lower third is minor (lower-case numeral). The diminished fifth is denoted by the superscript '°'.

   ii) The chord symbol shows the root note, plus 'dim' or a superscript '°', for example B D F = B dim. or B°. The symbol is in fact not fully definitive (see p. 98).

   iii) In figured bass it is shown as any other triad, except that with the minor form the raised root (leading note of key) is indicated, unless shown in the staff. The secondary triads extend the possibilities for harmonization:

MAJOR	1	2	3	4	5	6	7
	I	V	I	IV	I	IV	V
	IV	V⁷		V⁷	V		V⁷
	vi	vii°	iii	ii	V⁷	vi	vii°
		ii	vi	vii°	iii	ii	iii

There are now three alternatives for each melodic note or, for those embraced by the dominant seventh chord, four.

In the minor mode many possibilities arise from the undefined nature of the minor scale. Though in theory minor harmonies are extracted from the harmonic scale, melodies use the melodic forms also, and these must be taken into account in harmonization. The secondary triads in the three forms of minor scale are given in Ex. 91. One new type appears, predictably that consisting of two *major* thirds and bounded by an augmented fifth – the **augmented triad**. As with the diminished triad, the loss of the perfect fifth makes the chord unstable. It is symbolized as follows:

   i) Functional symbol: a superscript 'dash' is added to the degree-number of the chord, the latter being upper-case since the lower of the two thirds is major.

   ii) The chord symbol adds '+' or 'aug' to the root note or, loosely, any of the component notes. Thus C E G♯ = C+ or C aug. It is understood that the raised note is the fifth.

iii) In figured bass it is treated like any other triad, but the raising of the fifth must be shown where required.

Ex. 91

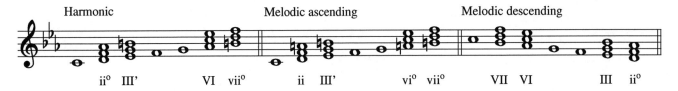

Concentrating for the moment on the less complicated major mode, we see how the primary and secondary triads are related:

		B			E			F
	G——G			C——C			D——D	
E——E——E			A——A——A			B——B——B		
C——C			F——F			G——G			
A			D			E			
vi	I	iii	ii	IV	vi	iii	V	iii°

On page 59, para. 6, we saw that chords may be related through common (shared) notes; the more shared, the closer the relationship. Each primary triad can be flanked by two secondaries, each sharing two common notes with it and thus closely related. Providing each contains a given melody note, this opens the way for a secondary triad to replace a primary in making a harmonization. If the melody note is the third of the primary triad, *two* substitutions are possible, for example I may be replaced by iii or vi.

An immediate application of this is in the deceptive cadence, where the expected tonic chord may make way for vi, as in Ex. 92*a*, before the music reaches the final tonic chord. It is possible to use iii in the same way, but as the shared notes do not include the tonic this is rarely done; a notional example is shown in Ex. 92*b*.

Ex. 92*a* (Handel)   ('Good King Wenceslas')

Ex. 92*b*

76

Substitutions may be made at almost *any* point in a piece of music, to secure variety and to get away from ponderous repetitions of I, IV and V, as in Ex. 75. We can now rework the same passage remembering that even *one* common note can establish a relationship between two chords, which opens up even wider vistas within these few simple bars. A revised version of Ex. 75 is shown in Ex. 93:

Ex. 93

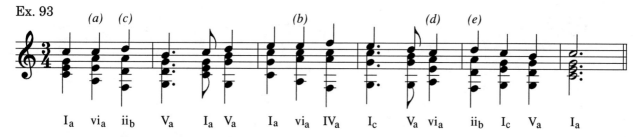

I_a vi_a ii_b V_a I_a V_a I_a vi_a IV_a I_c V_a vi_a ii_b I_c V_a I_a

i) To avoid immediate repetition of I, vi is used at (*a*) and (*b*).

ii) The whole phrase is of six bars; the final chord of bar 4 could easily give an impression of finality (the commonest length of phrase in music is four bars), albeit with a feminine cadence, whereas the phrase still has two bars to run. Use of vi at (*d*) avoids this, making a brief deceptive cadence.

iii) With the melody note as D we have the option of vii° or V at (*e*) ; trial will show them to be unsatisfactory. The alternative use of ii, which shares only the D with V, is much more effective, especially when in its first inversion, as at (*c*) and (*e*). At (*c*) it avoids also the use of V on *both* sides of the bar-line; a V at (*c*) weakens the force of V on the following, first beat.

Two important facts emerge:

1. Chords move strongly when their basses move downward by a third (or upward by a sixth). Note the effect of the bass progression (C to A to F) in bars 1 and 3, and in crossing from bar 4 to bar 5 (A to F).

2. The use of substituted secondaries often leads to a root-progression that follows the circle of fifths (p. 59), flowing with the tide. Thus in bars 1 and 3 the root progression becomes (C) to A to D to G (first beat of next bar) and, in passing from bar 4 to bar 5, A to D.

In Ex. 94 the dominant chords of Ex. 93 are extended to sevenths. That at D works well but the other three less so, weakening the effect in varying degrees. It is not *always* valid to replace a simple V with V7; in this piece the triad itself has a strength that fits the character of the melody. At B, for instance, the line of words ends with 'Queen' and the harmony rests better on it as V than as V7, which pushes forward too hard.

Ex. 94

Three more examples of substitution are given in Ex. 95, each together with the same passage with primaries instead of secondaries. The loss of variety and interest is easily heard. Note the deceptive cadence in Ex. 95a.

Ex. 95a (Handel)

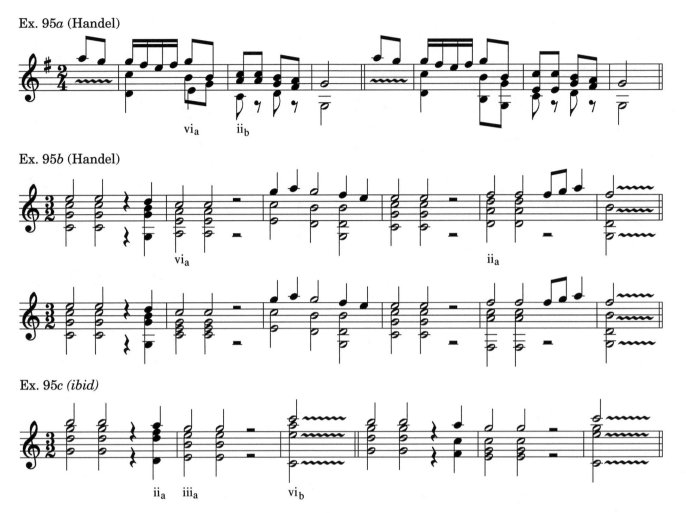

Ex. 95b (Handel)

Ex. 95c (ibid)

A balance between primaries and secondaries must be struck. The former assert and confirm the home key, while three of the latter (ii, iii, vi) are minor triads that weaken the feeling of the home (major) key – if used too freely they create ambiguity (e.g. C major or A minor?). In Ex. 96 a passage is shown with (a) too many secondaries, and (b) better balance.

Ex. 96a   Ex. 96b

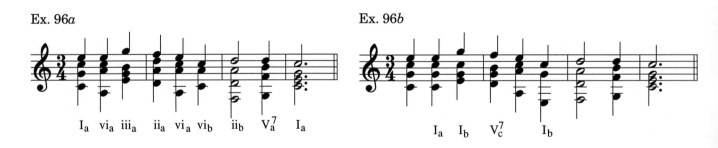

Note also, in Ex. 95b, how the secondary chords are quickly followed by confirmations of the home key. Beware of 'substitutionitis'; it can spread like measles.

The dominant seventh chord could be regarded as a 'telescoping' of the dominant and leading-note triads (Ex. 97):

Ex. 97

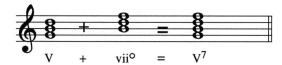

The chord vii° may be used in its own right, though usually to underline its association with dominant harmony – its tritone resolves the same way as in V7. Two examples, one minor and one major, are given in Ex. 98:

Ex. 98a (Bach)   Ex. 98b (Sor)

I-IV-V(7)-I

There are many formulae in harmonization, but that of I-IV-V-I is ubiquitous. It is a self-enclosed 'cell' of the three primaries defining a key and has a sort of symmetry: I acts as 'dominant' to IV, V(7) replies as dominant to I.

Ex. 99a (Bach)   99b (Sor)

Ex. 99c (Sanz)

Ex. 99d (Batchelar)

Ex. 99*e* (Coste)

Ex. 99*f* (Carcassi)

That of Ex. 99*a* is reduced to essentials (vii° incomplete, in place of V7) and the upper notes embellished with lower auxiliaries. The bracketed thirds in Ex. 99*b* are unaccented passing notes, the other two in each bar adding up to I, IV, V, I. In Ex. 99*c* the sequence is modified to stress iv, and the F♯ in bar 1 underlines its root (G). The stress is different again in Ex. 99*d*, the final I being only an upbeat chord to bar 3 (bars 3 and 4, not shown, lead back to I via IV and V7). Ex. 99*e* is the middle eight bars of a 16-bar section that begins with four bars firmly based on I (A minor); the melodic line has accented passing notes (*appoggiature*) at the asterisked points. Ex. 99*f* has IV replaced by ii♭ with an *appoggiatura* G♯ ending an eight-bar section.

In Exs. 99*a* and *b* the bass stays on the tonic note, regardless of the harmony above it. This device is known as a **pedal point**. In the present cases it helps to emphasize the key by keeping the tonic prominent. The harmonic tension is increased as I, IV and vii° appear successively over the tonic pedal, and is released when I returns. Bach was very fond of this device, and there are many examples of it in his music, for example the openings of Prelude VI ('48' Book I), and the Prelude of the Fourth Cello Suite.

Modulation and Transition

Changes of key often take place within a single movement or piece; the home tonic gives way to another tonal centre, for contrast and variety, giving pleasure when the original key is resumed.

1. Changes of key of this kind are of two types:
    i) a series of changes in harmony progressively obliterates the feeling of the first key and establishes that of another – *modulation*.

    ii) the change of key is made without preparation, a leap from one key to the other – *transition*.

2. To establish a key it is necessary to emphasize some feature characteristic of it and not of the previous one. The tritone between the fourth and seventh degrees is characteristic of a major scale (see p. 71, para 9), and strongly assertive in a minor one. Two keys are most closely related when their signatures differ by only one sign and they have, thus, six of their seven notes in common. If, from C major, we move to the two closest keys (F and G) we destroy the tritone of C major – B becomes B♭ or F becomes F♯, by the same process that establishes the new one – B♭/E or C/F♯. The tritone may belong to either V7 or vii°.

3. It follows from 2 that modulation cannot occur without the intrusion of at least one chromatic note.

4. Changes of key have various degrees of permanence:
    i) Familiarity with conventions plays an important role. In a small dance movement or a popular song one does not expect long stays in 'foreign' keys and, when the key changes, one knows it will not be for long, whereas in a sonata movement it may take some time to return to the 'home' key.

    ii) The longer and more decisive the process of changing key, the more important the change is made to feel, and the more it is likely to remain for some time.

    iii) A new key can be established through its tritone, but the more the change is reinforced by other chords characteristic of the new key, for example IV or ii, the more durable it will be. With transitions this is particularly important since there is no other way of obliterating the feeling of the old key, except by continuing unmistakably in the new one.

5. Changes may be divided into two types, according to the identity of the new key:
    i) **Simple** or **close modulation** (using the word in its broad sense of a change of key), to one of the two most closely related keys (dominant and sub-dominant), to the relative minor, or to the mediant or supertonic minor keys. Departing from C major, close modulation would thus be to G or F major, or A minor, E minor, or D minor. In the first chapter of the book we saw that, with unequal temperament, such as that which continued far into the baroque period, a keyboard would, with a given tuning, give its best (or least offensive) results if the music was confined to the key on whose tonic the tuning was based, or those most clearly related to it and sharing the most notes with it.

These six keys (I, IV, V, vi, ii, iii) formed a close-knit family and, for obvious reasons, much music of earlier times does not often venture outside it. The dance movements of Bach, Handel or Purcell, or the sonatas of Scarlatti show the high importance of close modulation. This conservatism, and the comparative technical ease of playing in closely related keys on the guitar, spilled over into the period of Carcassi, Aguado, Giuliani and others; Sor showed, however, a more adventurous spirit.

ii) **Extraneous** or **remote modulation**, to keys outside the family circle. Such modulations became freer and more important as equal temperament came into wide use and musical concepts changed.

The process of modulation can be lengthy and complex but we can, even at this stage, learn a great deal about it; neither do we need to go beyond the bounds of simple modulation.

1. *To the subdominant*
    i) The old tonic becomes the new dominant, for example C becomes dominant to F, and is easily established in its new role by adding the new seventh, e.g. C E G + B♭ becomes V7 in the key of F.

Ex. 100*a* (Diabelli)

ii) The new seventh is chromatic in the old key, and chords that contain it are also characteristic of the new key. Thus, in Ex. 100*b*, IV gives a positive feeling of the new key, two bars before the new V7 arrives.

Ex. 100*b* (Carulli)

2. *To the dominant*
    i) The introduction of the raised submediant note leads straight to the new V7.

Ex. 101 (Mozart)

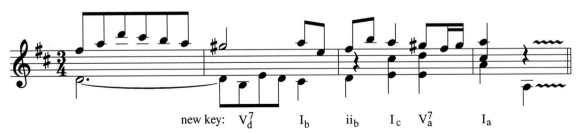

ii) The original I becomes IV in the new key, for example C becomes IV in the key of G, and supports the new V7.

iii) The chord of D major sketched by bar 1 of Ex. 101 'looks both ways', as I in the home key and IV in the new one (A major); the modulation turns on it like a hinge. Such a chord is termed a **pivot** or **nexus**, and is a very important tool in effecting changes of key. Here it is diatonic in both keys, in others it may be chromatic in either one or even in both.

iv) Modulation to the dominant key, establishing it as a temporary centre of contrast to the tonic, is common in many forms of music, for example hymns, carols, dance and folk music, sonatas, and pieces in binary form (see p. 43). When this occurs the journey is often made via the *dominant of the dominant*; in reaching G major from C major, for instance, we may establish D major, the dominant of G, itself the dominant of C.

3. *To the submediant (relative minor)*

   i) The raised dominant note provides the new leading note and therefore the way to the new V7.

Ex. 102*a* (Anon. Gigue)

ii) vi in the first key, which becomes i in the second, can also act as a pivot chord, diatonic in both keys. In Ex. 102*b* its identity as the new tonic chord becomes clear when, in the next bar, it is followed by its own iv (ii in the old key) and confirmed in the next bar when the expected D♯ appears. Owing to the close relationship between relative major and minor keys it is easy to plunge from one to the other, virtually as a transition, the possibly delayed appearance of the new V7 acting as confirmation rather than revelation of the key-change:

Ex. 102*b* (Sor)

Note: Ex. 102*b* is a further example of i-iv-V7-i; see p. 79.

iii) In Ex. 102*c* IV leads to ii (with *appoggiatura* G♯) and thence to the dominant of the new key F♯ minor; the following bars are clearly in that key. The old ii acts as the nexus.

Ex. 102c (Bach)

new key: iv i_c V_b
old key: ii

iv) A brief journey along the ascending melodic minor scale is enough to convey the impression of the coming key of vi, even though no harmony is yet involved:

Ex. 102d (Carulli)

new key: i_a V^7_b

Such preparation for change is possible in other key-changes (cf. Ex. 100b, where the D♮ in the first complete bar paves the way for A major, contradicting the leading note of the previous key).

4. *To the supertonic*

   i) The raised tonic note provides the tritone of the new key, G/C♯:

Ex. 103a (Sor)

   ii) The new key signature contains one note characteristic of the new key but foreign to the old, for example in changing from C major to D minor, a B♭. This note is contained in iv of the new key, in the above case, G B♭ D. The new iv can then lead smoothly into the supertonic key, adding to the effect of the new V.

Ex. 103b (Sor)

   iii) The original ii, also the new i, can act as a pivot chord. Though the home key of Ex. 103c is G major, the music at the beginning of the extract is firmly established in the dominant key (D), with its own dominant; the change is thus from I to ii (D to E minor), the asterisked chord being the nexus:

Ex. 103c (Carulli)

key D at this point

5. *To the mediant*

    i) This is perhaps the least common of close modulations; most often iii is approached through vi (which is iv in the new key). Ex. 104a is skeletal but clearly defined: the bracketed G and B♭ are enough to suggest vi (G minor) in the home key (B♭) and to act as a nexus, swinging the music towards D minor (iii), which is confirmed in the final bars.

Ex. 104a (Ponce)

    ii) The key of iii sometimes appears after a passage in the dominant key (for example home key C major, passage in G major leading to one in E minor), but this is really a I–vi modulation (from G) and not a I–iii (from C).

    iii) In Ex. 104b the approach is through a brief scale passage in the new key, the new tonic appearing as an appoggiatura over its dominant:

Ex. 104b (Ponce)

Returns to the original key, or shifts to other keys, may correspond to the above types (in reverse): for example the return from V to I may follow a I to IV course. Methods are legion, and it is impracticable to list them all, whether for an outward or inward journey.

MODULATING SEQUENCES

The establishment of a new key may be very brief and, even though the new tonic is supported by its own dominant harmony, it may carry no feeling of permanence. This is especially true of sequential passages in which a number of keys are touched upon in succession, often to provide a more interesting harmonization. Thus in Ex. 105a a sequence which nominally passes via iii and ii on its way back to I (each confirmed by its own dominant) is more interesting than that of Ex. 105b in which the harmonization stays rigidly in the home key. It does not however give any impression that these transient keys will be more than birds of rapid passage:

Ex. 105*a* (Traditional)

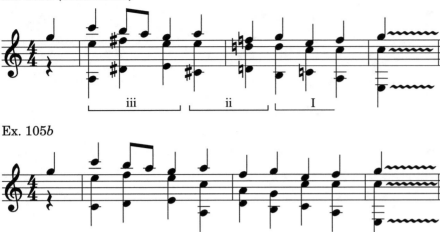

Ex. 105*b*

Further examples of such modulating sequences are given in Ex. 106, and it may be noted how they are matched by melodic patternings:

a) The first chord announces the arrival on the dominant of the dominant (D in the key of C). The sequence then touches the keys of G, F, E and D, the tonics stepping down the scale of the home key (a familiar pattern for a modulating sequence) and finally returns to C via its dominant seventh. The semitone drop (F to E) breaks the mechanical regularity and makes it easier to return home without too long a journey:

Ex. 106*a* (Sor)

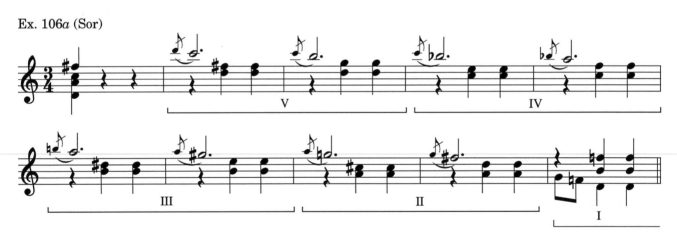

b) The music is in E minor, whose dominant leads to E major before the keys of A, D, G and C are touched in turn, following the circle of fifths. Though the writing is skeletal, references to the various keys are clear. The music is finally arrested and returned to the original key, the bass B (bar 3, beat 2) dismissing any notion that the sequence might continue into F major, the next key in line, in which a B♭ would be needed. The bass-note pattern within each bar forms a sequence in itself with the whole bar as the unit – E D C♯ A/D C B G/C B A F♯.

Ex. 106*b* (Bach)

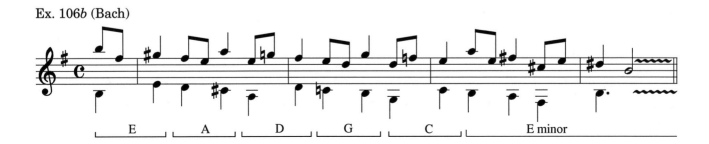

c) Villa-Lobos begins with a transition, from E major to the remote key of C major (a smooth and easy one – E is tonic of the first key and mediant of the second and, in a sense, acts as a pivot); the roots of the following chords move through the circle of fifths in the same way as Bach's (an extremely popular process), alternate chords being dominant sevenths, so that the keys of B♭, A♭, and F♯ are traversed *en passant*, an enharmonic change (G♭ = F♯) making it easier to resume the home key. The third semiquaver of each group of four is an *appoggiatura*. Experience teaches us to expect the return of the home key, the passing visits being brief, and it is firmly established when it does come, by continuing for some bars, halting the sense of sequence.

Ex. 106*c* (Villa-Lobos)

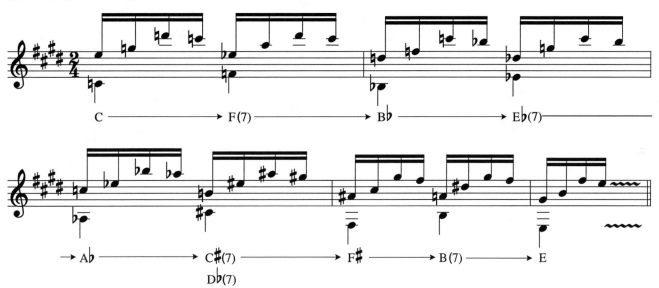

Modulating sequences are common in music, especially that of a popular nature, and much loved by guitar composers; their musical patterns are often reflected in fingering patterns. The three types shown (*a*) by diatonic step, (*b*) round the circle of fifths, starting from the home key, and (*c*) as (*b*) but starting from an extraneous one, are not the only possibilities. It is easy to identify many more instances; a small book could be filled with examples from Sor's music alone. Interest and diversion are created through the exploitation of a repeated, and usually easily identified, pattern, with transient references to other keys.

This by no means exhausts the possibilities for modulation, even within our present modest vocabulary. For instance, processes that lead clearly to closely related keys may also lead to more remote ones:

1. The principles of (*a*) reaching a new key through a nexus, and (*b*) confirmation of the new key by introducing its characteristic harmonies, remain valid whatever the 'target' key.

2. Arrival in a new key via its V or V7 may apply to either major *or* minor modes; for example, in leaving C major and moving via A(7) we can reach either D minor (ii), the near key, or D major (II), the more remote one. This may be seen in Ex. 106*a*.

Further discussion of modulation is better reserved, however, until our harmonic vocabulary is enlarged, the more since remote modulations came into freer use during times when more 'adventurous' harmonies entered the *lingua franca* of music.

Before continuing, we will take one further example, which shows remote keyshifts (transitions rather than modulations) using only chords we already know. The principle of the nexus can apply to single notes as well as chords, and many involve an enharmonic change of the pivot note itself. One of the simplest cases is that in which the original tonic note becomes the new leading note, so the key-centre rises by a semitone, inevitably a remote change. Ex. 107 follows a long passage clearly in the home key of D minor (and over a pedal note of D). At (1) the D becames the leading note of E♭; at (2) the new 'home' triad changes mode from major to minor; at (3) there is a double enharmonic change (E♭ = D♯ and G♭ = F♯), paving the way for (4) where E major arrives, suffers a similar change from major to minor mode and then, at (5), reading the B♮ as a Dorian sixth (see p. 66), naturally slips back into D minor via its dominant seventh, the 'minor' flavour of which is quickly established by reversion to a B♭ at (6). Here we have a brief but effective chain of transient modulations.

Ex. 107

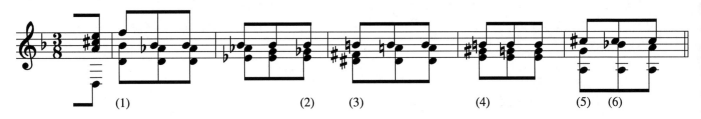

Secondary Sevenths

We have seen how new harmony may be derived naturally from commonplace harmony, by induction, stemming from melodic processes – by which means we explained the dominant seventh. More arbitrarily, we can arrive at the same chords by adding a diatonic third to the pile, a method described by Rameau in the eighteenth century. The same two methods can yield other diatonic chords of the seventh. In Ex. 108 there are parallels with Ex. 80, and the chords formed by inducting the passing notes (asterisked) are rewritten in their close-piled forms. That formed on vii° is, like the parent triad, a special case in that its fifth is imperfect; it will be considered separately.

Ex. 108*a*   Ex. 108*b*   Ex. 108*c*

Ex. 108*d*   Ex. 108*e*

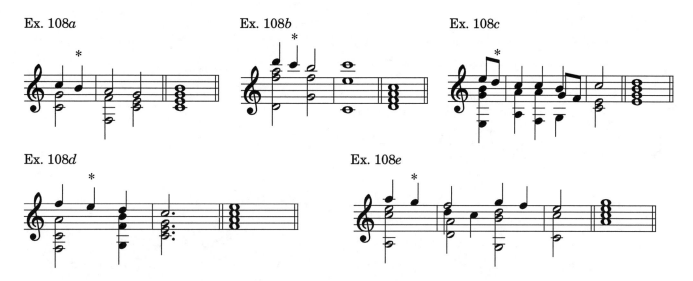

If these chords are ordered as in Ex. 109 they form a succession into which the dominant seventh fits neatly, and each chord could equally well be produced by adding a further third to the basic triad. These new chords (including that on the leading note, not shown) are termed the **secondary sevenths** of a key, and they subdivide into two groups:

Ex. 109

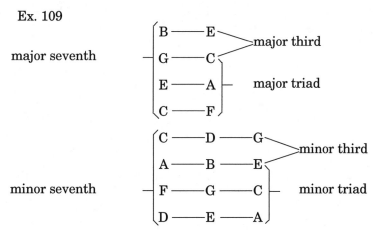

The major triads carry major thirds, the minor have minor thirds; the boundary intervals correspond in type.

1. The *secondary sevenths* are important chords, common in music since the Baroque period, and harmonic cornerstones in today's jazz and popular music.

2. *Symbolization*

   i) Functional symbols: the superscript 7 is added to the symbol for the basic triad, e.g. D F A/C in the key of C major = ii^7, C E G/B = I^7.

   ii) Chord symbols: The assumptions made in the case of the dominant seventh, i.e. that the triad is major, and the boundary interval a minor seventh, apply here also. The secondary-seventh chords based on a minor triad have '7' added to the triad symbol (*minor* seventh, understood) e.g. D F A C = Dm7 (or Dmi7 or Dmin7); those based on a major triad carry 'maj7' (or ma7) or the triad symbol, e.g. C E G B = Cmaj7 (or Cma7). In common parlance the former type is spoken of as a **'minor seventh'** chord, the latter as a **'major seventh'**, an imprecise but serviceable usage.

3. *Distribution*

   Some secondary sevenths can be played in their close-piled forms (Ex. 109) but on the guitar they are more often found in open or mixed spacings (Ex. 110).

Ex. 110

4. *Doubling and omission*

   Like the third, the seventh is a characteristic note and is, under most circumstances, better not doubled; the root is the best note to double. No note can be omitted without leaving an ambiguous residue, but if the fifth, or even the third, is left out the context will usually suffice to define the chord. If we are concerned only with 'major' and 'minor' sevenths there is no ambiguity in the absence of the fifth, but this does not hold for *all* types of seventh chord.

5. The secondary sevenths may be viewed as 'telescoping' of the primary triads with secondary ones that are potential substitutes for them (see pp. 77 ff):

		B	B			C	C				D	D	
G	G	G			A	A	A		B	B	B		
E	E	E	=	F	F	F	=	G	G	G	=		
C		C		D		D		E		E			

I + iii = I^7 ii + IV = ii^7 iii + V = iii^7

		E	E			G	G	
C	C	C		E	E	E	
A	A	A	=	C	C	C	=
F		F		A		A	

IV + vi = IV^7 vi + I = vi^7

90

They are mostly used in the same way as the triads of which they are extensions, whether primary or secondary. In some cases the distinction may be largely academic, for instance if ii^7 is followed by V^7 it is a course equally open to the two triads, ii or IV.

6. *Resolution*

   i) Neither the major nor the minor secondary seventh contains a tritone nor, accordingly, does it share the instability of the dominant seventh.

   ii) At the same time they do not share the restful consonance of the common chords. In the last century, however, we became quite accustomed to them in the cadential positions traditionally occupied by major and minor triads. Thus, Ponce disturbs no one when he ends with a tonic major seventh (Ex. 111*a*), especially since he has prepared the ground by stressing the leading note at the ends of preceding sections (Exs. 111*b* and *c*). This is in a sense an extension of the baroque practice of leaning heavily on the leading note at a cadence, the following tonic note being much less emphasized – which is halfway to ending with the tonic major seventh (Ex. 111*d*); the same convention is evoked in the ending given in Ex. 111e, which also has a *tierce de Picardie*.

   iii) In resolving, if we regard the secondary seventh as a dissonance, or merely passing to another chord, the notes of the basic triad may behave in the same way as if no seventh were present. The seventh itself may also follow its natural melodic tendencies, the subdominant of the home scale tending to fall, the leading note to rise by a semitone, when present as the seventh of the chord. Ex. 111*f* shows the leading note (A) both approached and quitted by a semitone step; Ex. 111*g* shows a more recent example of the same thing. The strongest tendency may however be resisted; in Ex. 111*h* the major seventh resolves downwards.

   iv) Secondary sevenths can form a 'chain' whose 'links' have roots that follow the circle of fifths, a two-link example being shown in Ex. 111*i*, vi^7 being substituted for I, which is used when the phrase first appears. Much more freedom is exercised on occasion, and secondary sevenths may simply replace the corresponding triads; this is illustrated in Ex. 111*j*, rewritten in k with triads in place of sevenths. They may also follow one another in diatonic procession, moving along the scale (Ex. 111*m*).

   v) In common with most other chords the secondary sevenths may be used in two ways: (1) as essential harmony – when the seventh itself is the melodic note, as in Exs. 111*a, c, e, h, n* and *o*; and (2) in support of a melody note present also in the basic triad, where the seventh is enclosed in the chord as 'decoration' or 'coloration'. In this sense even the third of a common chord may be viewed as a coloration of the perfect fifth. This form of use is exemplified in Exs. 111*f, g, j, m,* and on the first beat of bar 2 of *n*.

   vi) Secondary sevenths are more often than not used in root position, though exceptions such as those of Exs. 111*p* and *q* are not infrequent. Bach, an enthusiastic user of secondary sevenths, often produces inverted forms by making the bass line step down the scale (Exs. 111*r* and *s*) or by retaining the bass while changing the harmony above it (Ex. 111*t*) – as though embarking on a pedal point (see p. 80).

vii) We have noted that ii^7 may be regarded as the offspring of ii and IV, and may behave in a way proper to either 'parent'. If the more important parent is considered to be ii, the derivation is D F A/C, that of the secondary seventh. If however it is taken to be IV, the primary triad for which ii is a secondary substitute, the structure of the chord would be F A C/D, IV with a major sixth added above the root. This is the first of a variety of **chords of the sixth** we shall meet. It is symbolized by adding '6' to either the functional or chord symbol for the basic triad, e.g. F A C D = IV^6 or F6, the sixth being understood to be major. In figured bass the sixth is shown as diatonic and must be adjusted with an accidental where necessary. In Ex. 111p the asterisked chord could be described as ii^7_b but it would probably be more appropriate to view it as IV^6_b, the sixth being the melody note. Other examples are shown in Exs. 112a and b:

Ex. 111a (Ponce)

Ex. 111b (idem)

Ex. 111c (idem)

Ex. 111d (Scarlatti)

Ex. 111e (Martin)

Ex. 111f (Sor)

Ex. 111g (Ponce)

Ex. 111h (Tórroba)

Ex. 111i (Ponce)

Ex. 111j (Tansman)

I   iii^7 IV^7 iii^7

Ex. 111k

I   iii   IV   iii

Ex. 111m (Turina)

Ex. 111n (Duarte)

Ex. 111o (Tórroba)

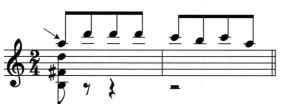

Ex. 111p (Handel)

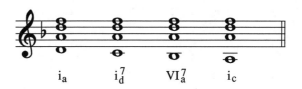

Ex. 111q (Ponce)

Ex. 111r (Bach)

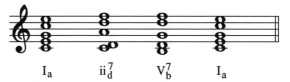

i_a i_d^7 VI_a^7 i_c

Ex. 111s (Bach)

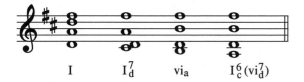

I I_d^7 vi_a $I_c^6 (vi_d^7)$

Ex. 111t (Bach)

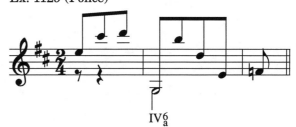

I_a ii_d^7 V_b^7 I_a

Ex. 112a (Castelnuovo-Tedesco)

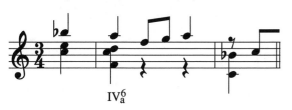

IV_a^6

Ex. 112b (Ponce)

IV_a^6

viii) A sixth may also be added to the tonic triad (I^6), the alternative face of vi^7, e.g. A C E/G becomes C E G/A, either as the melody note (Ex. 113a) or as a colorant (b) inside the chord. Chords formed by adding a sixth above the root of a common chord are termed **chords of the added sixth**. If the melodic line traverses the home scale from tonic through dominant, a succession of related chords is formed above tonic harmony (Ex. 113c):

Ex. 113a (Rosetta)

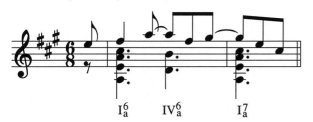

I_a^6 IV_a^6 I_a^7

Ex. 113b (L. Berkeley)

I_c^6

Ex. 113*c* (Villa-Lobos)

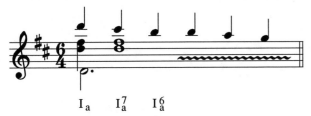

$$I_a \qquad I_a^7 \qquad I_a^{\,6}$$

7. *Secondary sevenths in the minor mode*

> i) The unpositive character of the minor mode is reflected in its secondary sevenths.

> ii) Among those formed within the harmonic minor scale (Ex. 114) we find a 'minor seventh' on the subdominant site, and a 'major' on the submediant. Both are frequently used, and an example of the former is given in Ex. 115.

Ex. 114   Ex. 115 (Bach)

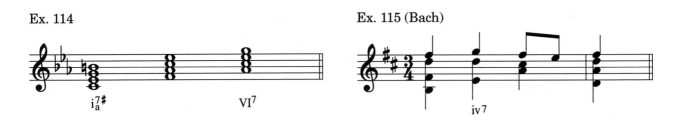

> iii) Only one other harmonic-minor secondary seventh has a perfect fifth above its root, the tonic seventh; this is a new type, with a major third added to a minor triad, and it completes the possible range of secondary sevenths:

added third:	minor	major	minor	major
basic triad:	major	major	minor	minor
chord type:	dominant	major	minor	minor-major

This new chord, with the faintly absurd common-parlance name of **'minor-major seventh'** (minor triad, added major third), is less used than its companions; it has an air of pathos. Though arising here on the tonic site, it may be based on any suitable degree of the scale, often involving accidentals in its notation – which, in any case, is common in the minor mode. Ex. 116 shows examples of this chord on tonic, supertonic and subdominant sites. The tonic form is also clearly implied in bar 1 of Ex. 111*c*, where the seventh falls, finally, to the dominant instead of rising to the tonic.

Its functional symbol is like that for the minor-seventh chord on the same root, with a sharp or natural sign (according to context) to show the raised seventh, e.g. A C E G♯ = $i_a^{7\sharp}$ in A minor. The chord symbol merely adds 'min. maj.' to the root name – the foregoing chord would be A min. maj.7.

Ex. 116a (Ponce)   Ex. 116b (Duarte)   Ex. 116c (Duarte)

To summarize:

1. Secondary sevenths may be produced by extending the triads on all scale notes other than the dominant by a diatonic third. Those on 1, 2, 3, 4 and 6 in the major scale, and 1, 4 and 6 in the minor (harmonic) have a perfect fifth above their root. They are of three types – minor, major, minor-major, according to the nature of the basic triad and of the added third.

2. Before the end of the nineteenth century they were regarded as dissonances that required preparation: the smooth way in which the ground is prepared is obvious in Exs. 111*f, p, r, s* and *t*, and equally in the later examples *e, g, h, j* and *q*. Our attitude to dissonance has changed radically since then; we no longer feel any pressing need to prepare dissonances, and we treat them more arbitrarily. Preparation may hardly exist in the earlier, strict sense, as witness Ex. 111*n* and, even more so, Ex. 112*b* and Exs. 116*a* and *b*, all of which are endings of the pieces quoted.

3. These three categories of secondary seventh can be thought of as compressions of the basic triad with that formed by the three highest of its notes; except for i^7 in the minor mode this represents a fusion of the primary triad with the upper of the two secondaries that may be substituted for it. Their behaviour in a sequence of harmony usually reflects that of the basic triad, the former acting as a decorated version of the latter. In the case of minor sevenths, in which the primary is the upper one of the two fused triads, there can be ambiguity and it is often more useful to view the chord as a decorated primary triad – a chord of the added sixth.

4. While the basic-triad notes normally move, in passing to another chord, as they would do with a plain triad, the seventh itself often follows its normal melodic course as a scale note. Thus it tends to rise if it is the leading note, or fall if it is the subdominant, though exceptions occur, as in Exs. 111*h* and *n* (bar 2). Other seventh notes often tend to fall rather than rise, as in Exs. 111*f, g, j,* and Ex. 115; but they do not always (see Ex. 113*a*).

5. The approach to and quitting of a secondary seventh may take two forms: (i) as part of a succession of different chords, and (ii) *en passant*, only one note changing in making the step, which is the direct product of melodic movement (see Exs. 111*r* and *s*, and Ex. 113*c*).

6. Successions, and even long sequences, of secondary sevenths often occur naturally, in which the root of the chord rises by a perfect fourth at each step (see Exs. 111*f* and *n*) and compare the behaviour of secondary triads (p. 77). In this vein, ii^7 moves strongly to V^7 (e.g. Ex. 111*f*) – and note the root progression in Ex. 115.

7. The seventh itself may be the melody note, and therefore essential to the harmony (e.g. Exs. 111*a, h* and *n*, Exs. 113*a, c,* and Ex. 116*b*), or it may be merely decorative, while the melody note belongs to the basic triad, as in most of the other related examples.

8. Secondary sevenths are most often found in root position, but exceptions occur. When a minor seventh is inverted a *double entendre* often arises and it is more appropriate to regard the chord as one of the added sixth.

9. The names 'major seventh', 'minor seventh' and 'minor-major seventh' are not in normal academic use, but they provide convenient labels and avoid some circumlocutions.

10. The root is usually the best note to double, the fifth or even the third is best to omit. Secondary sevenths are most often encountered on the guitar in open or mixed, rather than close distributions.

We must now look at the diatonic chords of the seventh which do not have a perfect fifth above their root, the bridge to our next step, beyond chords of the seventh.

Other Diatonic Secondary Sevenths

The most important are formed on the leading note of the major or minor scale, as in Ex. 117; they are sometimes referred to as **'leading sevenths'**.

Ex. 117

1. The tritone inherited from the parent triad, vii°, makes them essentially dissonant.

2. Though useable on its own, vii° has been seen as an incomplete dominant seventh; these leading sevenths are likewise incomplete forms of the dominant ninth, a chord we shall meet shortly. Their use usually reflects this relationship and they act as 'dominants' even though the dominant note is absent. The major form is less used than the minor; Ex. 118a shows it, sandwiched between two appearances of I^7 in a passage that might have been less interestingly written as in Ex. 118b. Ex. 119 shows two further examples of the major (a and c), and one of the minor form (b); it is often borrowed for use in a major climate where, strictly speaking, it is no longer a diatonic chord.

Ex. 118a (Tórroba)   Ex. 118b

Ex. 119a (Sor)

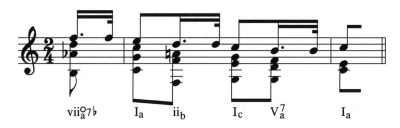

Ex. 119b (Bach)

Ex. 119*c* (Carcassi)

3. The minor form is unusual and important. Its boundary interval is a diminished seventh (in Ex. 117, B/A♭ = dim. seventh) and it is referred to as a **diminished seventh chord**.

    i) Each of its notes stands at a distance of three semitones from each of its neighbours :

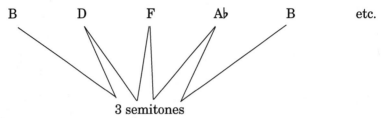

No one note is thus in a distinctive position, beyond that suggested by the musical context of the moment. The chord lacks aural shape and does not have the clear orientation of, say, a dominant seventh, even though it is a marked dissonance.

    ii) As a four-note chord it has a root position and three inversions, but all have the same aural effect; inversion does not alter its total symmetry. Played successively, the four positions of the chord sound 'aimless', lacking any distinctive starting or finishing point – in contrast to those of other chords we have met.

    iii) Only three different diminished-seventh chords are possible, for example those based on B, C and D♭.

    iv) In writing diminished sevenths **expedient notation** is often used for simplicity of reading. By this we mean that some notes may be shown in enharmonic forms, avoiding, for instance, double sharps or flats. While this does not, on the guitar at least, alter the sound, it is to be borne in mind when identifying these chords in a score.

    v) The diminished seventh has *two* tritones (B/F and D/A♭ in Ex. 117) and is thus acutely unstable. The lack of a clearly defined root, coupled with the fact that the two tritones 'point' in different directions, gives the chord a challenging and dramatic character. It has probably been the most overworked chord in all music during the last two centuries, especially in the romantic period, when dramatic gestures suited the climate of opera and *Sturm und Drang*. It is a tribute to its durability that it has not become cheapened beyond redemption.

    vi) The clearest symbols for the diminished seventh are 'dim7' (chord symbol system) or '°7' (chord or functional symbol), for example Gdim7 or G°7 (vii°7). Too often the symbol used is the same as that for the diminished triad (see p. 75), and confusion can result. In popular music a simple diminished triad is seldom envisaged and it is safer to read the chord symbol as calling for a diminished seventh.

4. The major form of leading seventh is, in inversion, capable of the kind of ambiguity already seen with the minor sevenths. In the first inversion, for example, B D F A becomes D F A B, showing a major sixth above the root of the triad – D F A/B, as with the major form, with the chord symbol Dm6. The major form of vii⁷ thus inverts to ii⁶, the sixth itself serving as either melody note or internal coloration. Examples are given in Ex. 120.

Ex. 120a (Duarte)

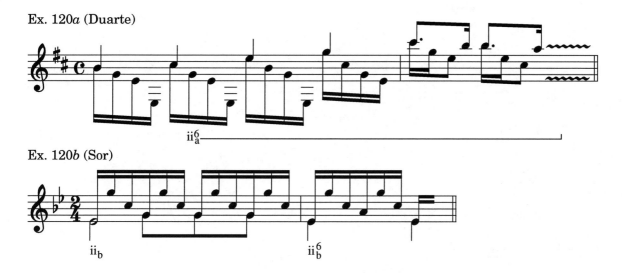

The same chord is equally at home, in the minor mode, on the subdominant site: for example in C minor (harmonic) ii⁷ is D F A♭ C which, when inverted, becomes F A♭ C/D = Fm6, the subdominant sixth of the key.

Ex. 121a (Sor)

5. The remaining secondary seventh in the minor mode is that on the mediant, e.g. E♭ G B D in C minor: colourful, looking to two keys at once (E♭ and G major) or, in its minor context, to tonic *and* dominant harmony. It is very little used.

The Cadential Six-four

Some of the many available ways of approaching the cadential six-four (p. 64) may be listed.

1. *From tonic harmony*

   The bass rises by a fifth (from root position) or a third (from first inversion): Ex. 103*b*, from I_a; Ex. 122*b*, from i_a; Ex. 122*a*, from i_b, via a passing chord – see 5, below.

Ex. 122*a* (Sor)

Ex. 122*b* (Bach)

2. *From supertonic harmony*

   The bass rises by a fourth (from root position) or by step (from first inversion): Ex.122*c*, from ii_a; Ex. 95*a* and Ex. 122*d*, from ii_b.

Ex. 122*c* (Sor)   Ex. 122*d* (Bach)

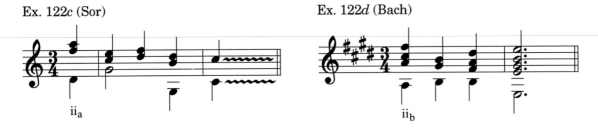

3. *From subdominant harmony*

   The bass rises by step (from root position), or falls by step (from first inversion): Ex. 111*d* and Ex. 122*e*, from IV_a; Ex. 122*f*, via IV_a^7 and IV_a^6; Ex. 122*g*, from iv_a^6; Ex.122*h* from iv_b^6.

Ex. 122*e* (Sor)

Ex. 122*f* (F. Couperin)

Ex. 122*g* (Sor)

Ex. 122*h* (L. Couperin)

4. *From dominant harmony*

When V is in root position the bass is already prepared: Ex. 100*b*, from V_a^7.

5. The passing chord (D B D) in Ex. 122*b* is incomplete and could represent several possibilities. In Ex.122*i* a very similar passage in the major mode allows longer for the effect of this residue to register; in this it seems to lack an F♯ and to be an incomplete ii$_b$ with the third doubled. It is in any event the natural result of contrary motion between bass and treble parts in each case:

Ex. 122*i* (Sor)

6. *From the dominant of the dominant*

This is, strictly speaking, supertonic harmony and a chromatic chord in the key concerned, but is perhaps worth listing separately. Its potency lies in the approach to the dominant note, in the bass, by a leading note. Ex. 122*j* shows this, the D♯ itself following a D♮, the dominant of the dominant thus being a passing chord:

Ex. 122*j* (Sor)

The leading seventh of the dominant key (generated by the dominant, see p. 97, para. 2) often replaces the dominant of the dominant, the bass again approaching the home dominant as a leading note; see Ex. 122*k* – in the preceding passage the A♮ is *not* approached from A♭, unlike Ex. 122*j*. In Ex. 122*l*, both leading (diminished) seventh and six-four chords are decorated with an appoggiatura (G♯ and F♯):

Ex. 122*k* (Sor)

Ex. 122*l* (Sor)

Most other methods of approach are based on these archetypes, through chromatic modifications of the same chords.

The Dominant Ninth

The dominant seventh chord may be extended to a chord of the ninth by adding a further third.

Ex. 123

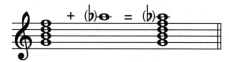

This has two forms, major and minor, according to the scale with which it is associated:

Ex. 124

These have the structures

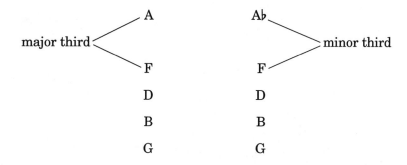

1. *Symbolization*

    i) Functional symbols: A superscript '9' added to the symbol for the basic triad, e.g. GBDFA in the key of C major = V^9; in C minor it would have the same symbol, the context of the minor scale making it clear that the A is flat

    ii) Chord symbols: The underlying seventh is assumed to be that on the dominant (a minor seventh above the root), the symbol for the above example being G9. As chord symbols are unaffected by musical context, the symbol for the minor form is thus G7♭9 or G7–9 (lowering is often represented by a minus sign, and raising by a plus). The '7' indicates the highest unaltered degree.

2. The ninth itself may either rise to the leading note of the scale (Ex. 125a) or, just as often, fall to the dominant (which is also the root of the chord itself) as in Ex. 125b. The latter tendency is more potent when the ninth is in the minor form and the step a semitone.

Ex. 125a   Ex. 125b

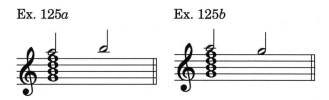

3. When the ninth rises the third of the chord is often omitted (Ex. 126a), avoiding a doubled third in the resolution; when it falls the root is left out (Ex. 126b) as its presence pre-empts the resolution. Though the ninth usually resolves by step, as above, it may also rise directly to the tonic in resolving, as in Ex. 126c:

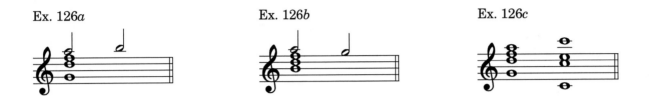

Ex. 126a   Ex. 126b   Ex. 126c

4. The dominant ninth is most often used incomplete – omission of the root produces the chord of the leading seventh (p. 97). This is particularly so in guitar music where the presence of so many notes can lead to difficult fingering. Examples of incomplete ninths are given in Ex. 127:

Ex. 127a (Duarte)   Ex. 127b (ibid)

Ex.127c (ibid)

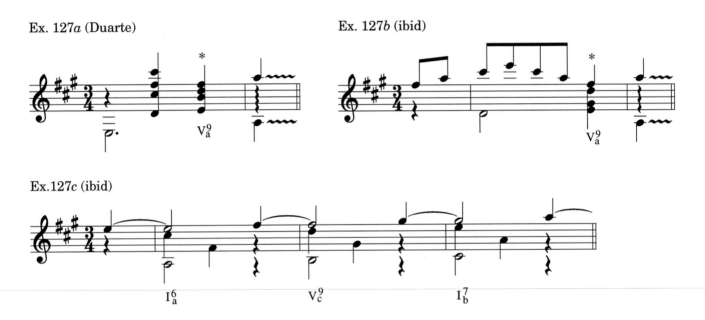

Ex. 127a lacks its third; b has no fifth, and c omits the root and is thus readable also as vii_b^7. The identification of residues from large chords is not always a simple question of rearranging the notes in optimum order. In the music from which Ex. 128 is taken the preceding context establishes an *ostinato* accompaniment in which chords of A major (I_a) and B minor (ii_b) alternate; when the E enters in the upper line the resulting chord is thus to be seen as a derivative of ii and not as v_d^7. The dominant ninth occasionally appears in its complete form in guitar music, but rarely – as in Ex. 129, showing minor and major forms in that order:

Ex. 128 (Rosetta)

Ex. 129a (Absil)

Ex. 129b (Ravel)

5. The characteristic note, the ninth itself, may appear either as the melody note, as in Ex. 127, or as coloration within the chord, as in Ex. 130.

Ex. 130a (Duarte)

Ex. 130b *(ibid)*

Ex. 130c *(ibid)*

Ex. 130d (Rosetta)

Ex. 130a lacks its third, b has no fifth, c has neither fifth nor seventh (though the latter is sketched in by the inner part *en passant*), and d shows the minor form of the chord without its seventh.

6. A complete dominant ninth in close position is difficult to play on the guitar, and may be discounted as a practical reality. Even in music written for other media the dominant ninth is most often incomplete. Any note except the ninth may be omitted without undue ambiguity, identity being implied by context. As with simpler chords, the characteristic note (the ninth) is not usually doubled, nor are the others, the third and seventh. The preceding examples show dominant ninths in a variety of compositions and distributions, acting in a typical 'dominant' role, preceding tonic harmony.

Secondary Ninths

Chords of the ninth may be similarly formed on the remaining degrees of the scale. Those produced within the major and the three minor scales are:

Ex. 131

The possibilities are numerous since either a major or a minor third may be added to any of the five remaining types of diatonic seventh chord – 'major', 'minor', 'minor-major', and the major and minor leading sevenths, and most of these are to be found in Ex. 131. Many are, however, difficult to handle, or aggressively dissonant, and are rarely used, for example on the third and seventh degrees of the major scale, so that the repertoire of chords of the ninth is, in practice, smaller than it at first seems.

1. Complete secondary ninths are seldom used, being as hard to manage on the guitar as is the dominant ninth.

2. They appear most often in open and mixed spacings, with one or more notes omitted. The ninth itself may resolve upward (to the third) or downward (to the root). When it is merely decorative it most easily moves by step to a note in the next chord, but considerable freedom is often exercised in this.

3. Composers have long used chords of the ninth as *appoggiatura* chords, but in the nineteenth century they became very popular, both for their colourful sound, and because the *appoggiatura* itself provided a way of 'pausing' with a dramatic gesture (some writers have even claimed that this often retarded the flow of the music excessively).

4. When both the ninth *and* its resolution notes are present, especially the third, the *appoggiatura* effect of the ninth is weakened. Either fifth or third may be omitted, usually without creating ambiguity, but the root cannot, since the residue would simply be a 'higher' chord of the seventh: e.g. D F A C E (ii$^9_8$ in C major) would become F A C E (iv^7_a). The same factor affects both chords of the seventh (e.g. F A C E becomes A C E = vi$_a$, continuing the previous example), and more extended diatonic chords.

5. In general, secondary ninths may be treated as more colourful versions of the parent secondary sevenths.

Ex. 132*a* (Ravel)

Ex. 132*b* (Duarte)

Ex. 132c (Fox)

Ex. 132d *(ibid)*

Ex. 132e (Duarte)

Ex. 132f (Ravel)

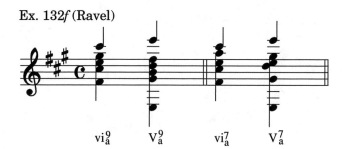

a) I_a^9 (no fifth): the ninth is a melodic note and resolves by upward step.

b)   Complete I_a^9 used as final chord despite its mild dissonance, and preceded by iv_a^9 (no third) to give a form of plagal cadence.

c) i_a^9 (no seventh) : the ninth is a decorative note and is not formally resolved.

d)   The ninth is again harmonic, but steps up to another chord note (A), which then resolves on to the third.

e)   Complete ii_a^9, preceded by I_a^9 (fifth omitted), which resolves on to I_a^6 (no fifth).

f) vi_a^9 (no third): the ninth is a colorant note and steps down to the ninth of the next chord (V_a^9); the chords could have been written as the corresponding sevenths (vi^7, V^7), but less colourfully.

6.   Secondary ninths are normally found in root position, as in all the foregoing examples.

THE ADDED NINTH

A simple triad may carry a major sixth above its root, either as a decorative note or as an *appoggiatura*; the ninth is often used in the same way, the chord being described as one of the **added ninth**.

Ex. 133a (Duarte)

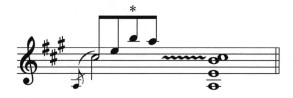

Ex. 133b (Sor)

107

Ex. 133c (Reusner)

Ex. 133d (Castelnuovo-Tedesco)

Ex. 133e (Ponce)

Ex. 133f (Ravel)   Ex. 133g (Duarte)

Ex. 133h (Tórroba)

a) The movement opens with the tonic chord, with the ninth as a brief *appoggiatura*; it ends with the chord shown, with the ninth as a colorant.

b) The ninth above the (tonic) chord is a strong *appoggiatura*.

c) The prevailing key is F major. The ninth enters as a suspension and leads to I_b on resolution.

d) In a succession of *appoggiature*, the ninth is used above tonic and subdominant harmony (first and third links in the chain).

e) Another chain of *appoggiature*, some aggressively dissonant; all are resolved.

f)   Ninth added to vi$_a$.

g)   Purely decorative ninths added to IV and I, not requiring resolution.

h)   Decorative ninth added to I. That on IV is immediately resolved, but returns – only to fall directly to the third of I$_a^9$.

The added ninth is now acceptable in the final chord of a piece of conventional music; in Ex. 133*i* the ambiguity of the final chord (third omitted) reflects the character of the preceding music, and in *j* the ninth is added to a minor triad despite its even greater dissonance.

Ex. 133*i* (Badings) Ex. 133*j* (Stoker)

The simultaneous addition of sixth and ninth to a triad has become commonplace in jazz and light music; it may also be found in 'art' music.

Ex. 134*a* (Blyton)   Ex. 134*b* (Absil)

Ex. 134*c* (L. Berkeley)

a)   deliberately evokes the association with jazz of pre-war, 'mainstream' vintage.

b)   takes advantage of the fact that a *barré* over the top five strings gives a ready-made chord of this type, needing only the root in the bass to anchor it (C♯ is the sixth, F♯ the ninth); the music is in the minor mode, so this last chord is also a *tierce de Picardie*.

c)   The ninth and sixth are introduced and immediately resolved downward, in turn; the effect of a chord of the added ninth and sixth is cumulative in the memory.

Chords of the Eleventh and Thirteenth

The methods of adding diatonic thirds and the induction of unessential notes are available to give even further extended chords, the elevenths and thirteenths. In theory it is possible to continue beyond this, but, as the fifteenth repeats the root (the double octave) it merely starts the whole cycle all over again. By merely piling up thirds of *any* kind it is possible to arrive at a chord in which all twelve possible semitones are used; the resulting harmonies are not usually considered in the conventional study of music and would in any case have limited application in that written for an instrument capable of producing only six notes at one time. The diatonic elevenths and thirteenths are shown, in close (and unplayable) position in Ex. 135; As and Bs may of course be flat in those chords derived from the minor scales: ( ) = thirteenth:

Ex. 135

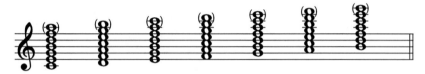

1. A chord of the thirteenth, with seven different notes, obviously *cannot* be played on the guitar in its complete form; though possible in limited ways, complete elevenths are also uncommon. IBANEZ 7 STRIN

2. To each of the types of chord of the ninth may be added a perfect eleventh and either a major or minor thirteenth, according to context. In practice however it would require a long search to find one example of many of them in guitar music. Of those used, the most important are those built on the dominant.

3. As with chords of the ninth, elevenths and thirteenths may be treated as more colourful forms of the seventh chords of which they are extensions. The eleventh and/or thirteenth note(s) may be either melodic or harmonic.

4. *Doublings and omissions:* The characteristic notes are not usually doubled, though, with such extended chords, the need seldom arises in guitar music. The root cannot be omitted without changing the status of the chord, but the third or fifth may be. The third is normally omitted from a chord of the eleventh since it clashes with the eleventh, especially in the major form; the eleventh is often dropped from a chord of the thirteenth.

5. *Symbolization:* Similar to that of sevenths and ninths, for example G B D F A C = G11 or V^{11} in C major, and G B D F A C E = G13 or V^{13} in the same key. Where the thirteenth is minor, the fact must be shown as before, by adding a flat sign or a "−" to the 13, and detaching this from the rest of the symbol (cf. p. 103, para. 1 (ii)).

110

6.

Ex. 136a (Castelnuovo-Tedesco)   Ex. 136b (Tórroba)

Ex. 136c (Duarte)   Ex. 136d (Sor)

Ex. 136e (Duarte)

Ex. 136f (Blyton)   Ex. 136g (Duarte)

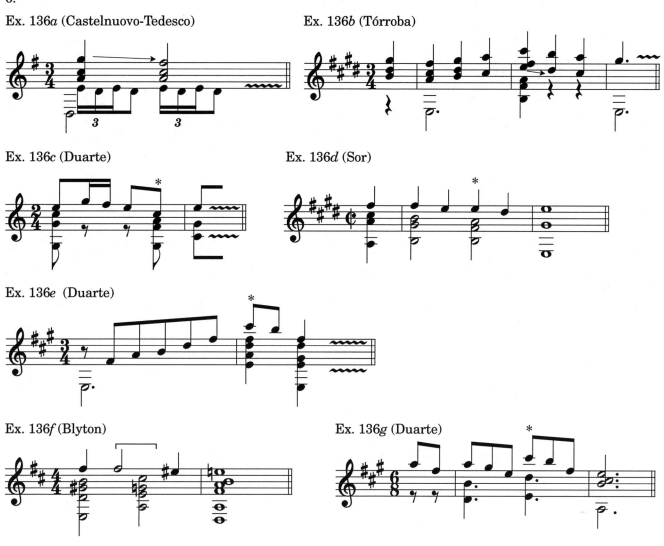

a) V^{11} (no third): the eleventh is a melodic note and resolves on to the third, the ninth finally resolves on to the root.

b) V^{11} (no third): the eleventh is decorative and, in bar 2, resolves on to the third, again together with the ninth (E and C♯ → D♯ and B).

c) V^{11} (neither third nor fifth): the eleventh is melodic and is disposed of by leap.

d) V^{11} (neither third nor ninth): the eleventh is melodic and resolves formally on to the third.

e) V^{13} (no third): the thirteenth is melodic and resolves normally on to the fifth; the eleventh, inside the chord, also resolves on to the third. The first bar arpeggiates the chord of the dominant eleventh (minus its third) and the last chord shown is the dominant ninth, lacking its fifth. The whole thus amounts to an elaboration of the dominant seventh – eleventh, thirteenth and ninth.

f) V^{13} (neither ninth nor eleventh): the thirteenth is melodic, arriving as a suspension and departing downward chromatically.

g) V^{13} (no third, fifth, ninth or eleventh): though the chord is skeletal its identity is made clear by the root, seventh and thirteenth. The (melodic) thirteenth resolves by downward step in the usual way.

Ex. 136*h* (Rosetta)   Ex. 136*i* (Pedrell)

Ex. 136*j* (Tórroba)   Ex. 136*k* (Sor)

While it is impossible to present a whole chord of the thirteenth on the guitar , it may be delivered piecemeal:

h)   Extended chords often occur over a pedal point. Successive use of iii, IV and V above a dominant pedal produces the cumulative effect of a complete V^{13}.

i)   The effect of the whole bar is of a complete V^{13}, as in *h*.

j) V^{13} (no third, fifth or eleventh) is established on the first beat; the third arrives on the second.

k)   Arpeggiation produces the effect of a complete V^{13}, unambiguously, though the first five notes could be read as V^9 and the next five as ii^9, a kind of *double entendre* common with extended harmony.

7.   An *appoggiatura* eleventh with V^7 such as that in Ex. 136*d* is commonplace. It is often used with the plain triad on any site, when it usually displaces the third, which appears when the resolution comes, and it is often referred to as the fourth, i.e. C F G = C/4 in chord-symbol language, though its correct identity, fourth or eleventh, depends on the context.

1. The fourth/eleventh may be either melodic or harmonic and may simply resolve to leave the triad itself.

Ex. 137*a* (Holborne)   Ex. 137*b* (L. Couperin)

Ex. 137c (Sor)

Ex. 137d (Sor)

Ex. 137e (Tórroba)

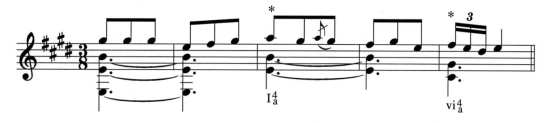

Ex. 137f (Sor)

Ex. 137g (Bach)

a)   The fourth appears briefly as an auxiliary note, and is decorative.

b)   The eleventh is melodic and is strongly stressed in a cadence that is very typical of the composer.

c)   The G (upper part) of bar 2 is obviously an *appoggiatura* even though the chord (iv) lacks its fifth. In the next bar another eleventh enters as a suspension (A) held over from I_c. The first is melodic, the second harmonic.

d)   Two *appoggiatura* fourths (decorative) lend tension to the peaks of a sequential phrase.

e)   In each case the resolution of the *appoggiatura* eleventh makes (melodic) use of *note cambiate*.

f)   An *appoggiatura*, melodic eleventh with (unusually) the third also present, resulting from melodic movement over stationary harmony.

g)   Similar to *f* but involving a double *appoggiatura* sequence above ascending thirds. Again the third and eleventh are simultaneously sounded; note the abrasive effect of the cross-relation of G natural in the treble line and the G sharp in the bass.

2.   The resolution of the *appoggiatura* fourth/eleventh may be accompanied or followed by the conversion of the triad to a dominant seventh, strengthening the cadential effect:

Ex. 137*h* (Sor)

Ex. 137*i* (Dowland)

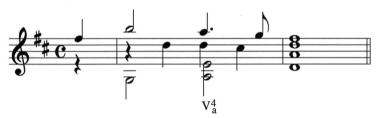

Ex. 137*j* (Holborne)

h)   The passage is skeletal but the status of the C in bar 3 is clearly that of an *appoggiatura* fourth, and the seventh appears on the last beat of the bar. The passage is sequential.

i)   The seventh itself appears briefly as a melodic passing note.

j)   Similar to *i*, but the seventh is introduced harmonically, just before the final resolution of the eleventh; both this resolution and that of the final bar involve *nota cambiata* effects (cf. Ex. 137e).

Chromatic Alteration of Diatonic Chords

The process of induction may be extended to take in chromatic notes, which are inessential by definition, as in Ex. 138, to produce a wide variety of new harmonies. Some are of course equivalent to so-called 'borrowings' from the minor for use in the major mode, and vice versa, for example the first example would have A♭ in the minor mode, as a diatonic note.

Ex. 138

1. The strong backbone of the common chord is the perfect fifth; if this is chromatically altered its strength is undermined – if it is diminished it becomes a tritone, the most unpositive of all intervals.

2. If the fifth of a major triad is raised, the resulting chord is termed an augmented triad (p. 75) . The triad family is:

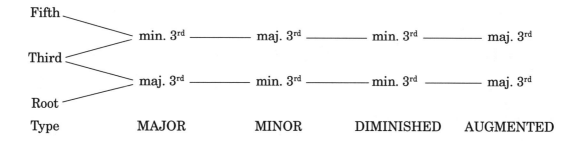

The augmented triad has exactly the same harmonic 'flavour' in all its three positions, since each degree is four semitones distant from each of its neighbours:

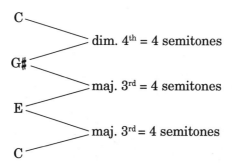

It thus has something in common with the diminished seventh chord, in which adjacent notes are separated by three semitones. The same quality of vagueness is shared by the product of *every* method of dividing the octave into equal steps:

12 x 1 semitone (chromatic scale)

6 x 2 semitones (whole-tone scale)

4 x 3 semitones (diminished seventh chord)

3 x 4 semitones (augmented fifth chord)

2 x 6 semitones (the tritone)

Despite this the chord is usually clearly oriented within a particular musical context.

3. The augmented triad occurs naturally in two forms of the minor scale (p. 75) but in the major mode it is always chromatic and is most often found on the tonic and dominant.

4. When one major triad follows another whose root is a perfect fourth higher, there is a stronger 'magnetic' pull if its fifth is augmented, thus providing *two* leading notes; the augmented triad then acts as a surrogate dominant seventh:

Ex. 139

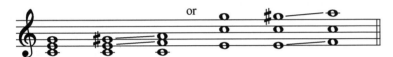

Ex. 140a (Sor)

Ex. 140b (Haydn)

Ex. 140c (Ponce)   Ex. 140d (Ponce)

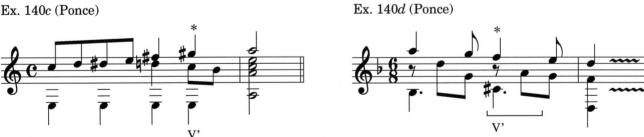

Ex. 140e (Ponce)

116

a)   At this point the (dominant) key of F major is firmly established. The augmentation of I enhances the I-IV progression

b)   Augmented triads on both I (leading to IV) and V (leading to I).

c)   Augmented triad formed, in passing, by contrary scale movement in the upper parts.

d)   Augmented triad resulting from scale movement in one part only, in a minor key, and followed by V7.

e)   A V-I relationship, but the second chord (bar 2) is a dominant eleventh, the *appoggiatura* eleventh itself acting as a *nota cambiata* in the resolution.

5.   An augmented triad may be formed, in passing, by chromatic movement in one or more parts. In Ex. 141*a* movement is in one part only, in *b* and *c* it is in two.

Ex. 141*a* (Castelnuovo-Tedesco)

Ex. 141*b* (Castelnuovo-Tedesco)

Ex. 141*c* (Duarte)

6.   Since an augmented triad is aurally 'symmetrical' any two of its notes may act as leading notes; it may thus behave as a nexus in key-changes. In bar 3 of Ex. 142 (the passage begins in F major) the tonic triad is augmented and, by enharmonic change (F becomes E♯), leads smoothly to D major.

Ex. 142 (Castelnuovo-Tedesco)

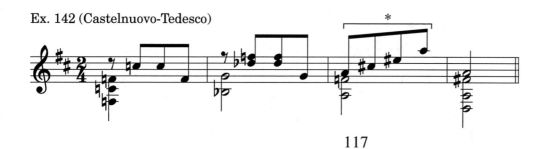

117

7. In Ex. 143, passing notes bridge the gaps between the chord notes, producing the effect of a whole-tone scale and even of a passing augmented triad. The effect of suspense suits the subject of the music:

Ex. 143 (Duarte)

8. If the fifth of a minor triad is augmented the resulting chord sounds identical with the first inversion of the related major triad VI, e.g. C E♭ G♯ = C E♭ A♭.

9. The fifth of a common chord may also be diminished. If it is a minor triad the result is simply a diminished triad, e.g. D F A♭ ; if it is major a new chord is produced, though it is seldom used – Ex. 144 shows one example:

Ex. 144 (Duarte).

10. The fifth of a chord of the seventh (usually the dominant seventh) may also be augmented or diminished:

Ex. 145a (Turina)   Ex. 145b (Duarte)

Ex. 145c (Turina)   Ex. 145d (Tórroba)

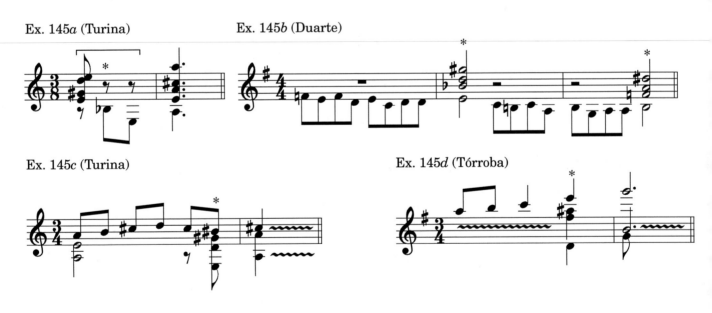

Ex. 145e (Duarte)

11. The higher degrees of more extended chords (ninth-thirteenth) may also be treated in the same way to produce a wide range of colourful harmonies that have become, since the late 1940s, the stock-in-trade of jazz and light music, as well as enhancing the art music of the romantic period. Again, chords on the dominant are most often concerned. Whole-tone steps in the movement of parts during a progression or resolution may be converted, by chromatic alterations, into semitones; these new leading and/or leaning notes make smooth connections between chords, the silky effect of chromatic harmony.

Ex. 146a (Pujol)

Ex. 146b (Duarte)

Ex.146c (Duarte)

Ex. 146d (Burkhart)

Ex. 146e (Ponce)

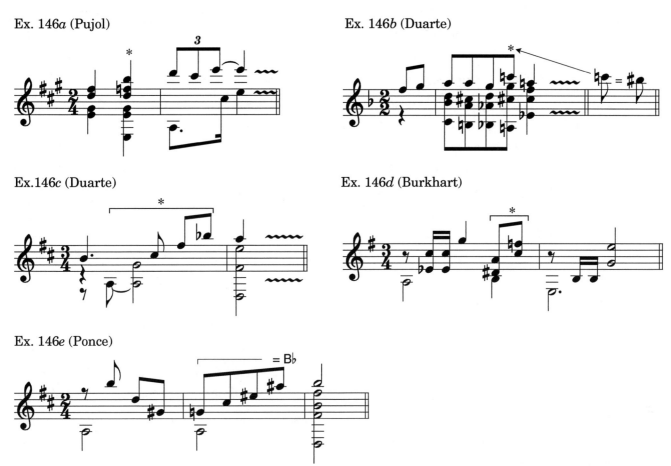

12. Chords altered in this way may also be regarded as being produced by the induction of chromatic passing notes (Ex. 147). With the intake of chromatic passing notes the process of induction reaches the limit of its capabilities in this form. That is not to say that the instances given represent the whole of chromatic harmony; it is simply that nothing beyond chromatic notes remains to be inducted.

Ex. 147

119

Chromatic Harmony

The terms 'diatonic' and 'chromatic' are less clearly defined than might at first appear:

   i) The advent of a B♭ in a piece whose home key is C major may signify a modulation to F major in which, no matter how brief the change of key, it is diatonic. This note may be regarded as being either diatonic or chromatic, according to one's viewpoint. Where modulation is established, as defined on pp. 81 ff., it is more realistic to regard the 'native' chords of the new key as diatonic, rather than to describe them in terms of the old one. This is the approach adopted in this book.

   ii) What is or is not diatonic in a major key is clear; in the case of a minor it is not. The three forms of minor scale are honoured more in the textbooks than in the reality of music; but the works of Bach show all three forms used in all three alleged functions. It is hard to say which form of the sixth or seventh degree is truly diatonic in many situations; in others it can be an academic exercise of dubious value. The term 'Dorian sixth' for a raised sixth degree reflects its historical origin but, as it is so often and naturally followed by a raised seventh degree – which might be attributed to the distant influence of *musica ficta* – it is simpler to relate it to the use of the melodic ascending scale, which is what it really is. In the handling of music we are not *obliged* to label a chord as 'diatonic' or 'chromatic'; it is more important to learn how to use it and to gauge its aural effect.

   iii) The inferences of (i) and (ii) above are reflected in the ways in which chords are symbolized in this book. The modern chord-symbol system, taking no account of context, describes a chord as well as it can, for what it is, and is thus more or less self-regulating in that the symbols take no account of whether a chord is chromatic in its context or not. The basic symbols adequately describe chords up to and including the sevenths, but in those that are more extended it is necessary to define the higher degrees, for example whether the ninth is major or minor: here the norm is the chord in its major-key situation, and deviation from this is shown. Thus G B D F A = G9, the major form being the reference standard, and G B D F A♭ = G7-9 (or 9♭), showing the lowered ninth. The highest unaltered degree of the chord immediately follows the name of the root, followed by the altered degrees in order, e.g. G B D♭ F A♭ = G7-5-9. In this book the same principle is applied to functional chord symbols, the root letter being replaced by the functional number so that, in C major, the above chord would be V7-5-9 or V7 5♭ 9♭.

A chord may be chromatic:

1. uncompromisingly, in *any* key, e.g. V7-5.

2. by virtue of its context, e.g. the triad C E G, though diatonic in C, F and G majors, is chromatic in D or A major.

When modulation takes place, chromatic notes and chords automatically appear. During the life of the new key such notes are diatonic in it, though they remain 'chromatic' in the old key. Any chord used in *reaching* the new key may fairly be regarded as chromatic even though it may become diatonic in the new key when this is established. Likewise, any such chord involved in quitting this new key remains chromatic until another key is set up.

The presence of chromatic chords does not of course imply that modulation has occurred, or even that it is about to do so; the word merely describes the status of the chord in its context.

Ex. 148 shows some of the many available uses of familiar triads, chromatic in their contexts but with no suggestion of a change of key. They appear for the sake of their colourful effect and element of surprise:

Ex. 148a (Tárrega)

The gentleness of the alternation between I and ♭VI prepares the ear for the minor form of the final plagal cadence (iv-I).

Ex. 148b (Castelnuovo-Tedesco)

The same juxtaposition as in a (♭VI-I) is used, but at the close, where it has a similar, peaceful effect to that of a plagal cadence. The reason for this is parallel in that the two chords concerned share the tonic note.

Ex. 148c (Duarte)

The sharing of a common note, the tonic, is the basis of this closing section – the tonic note is the root of i, the third of ♭VI and the fifth of IV.

Ex. 148*d* (Ponce)

The home key is D minor, but at this point the chord of C major in the first bar declares F major. In the next two bars this chord is juxtaposed with ♭II in the new key (♭IV in the old), the roots of these two being a tritone apart (C and G♭) and thus contrasting as strongly as possible, despite which 'remote' interruption the change from the chord of C to that of F remains smooth.

Ex. 148*e* (Duarte)

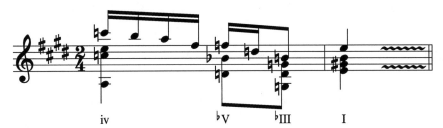

At this point the key of E minor, rather than E major, has been stressed, so the first chord is comfortably diatonic. The following chord (B♭ major) is a tritone distant from the base of E (cf. Ex. 148*d*) but the gap is bridged by the next chord (G major). The progression of the roots of the four chords is thus: A–B♭–G (3 semitones) –E (3 semitones) and, though it moves firmly, it does not 'challenge' the tonic as key-centre.

Ex. 148*f* (Ponce)

Two chromatic chords (VII and v) are connected by one leading and one leaning note; as the music up to this point has been purely diatonic, they come as a surprise. The first (C♯ major) might, in this context, be expected to lead to F♯ minor (mediant minor of D major) but only the G♯ moves in the expected direction; the other two notes slide down a semitone to give a chord of A minor, which is chromatic in this situation.

Ex. 148*g* (Ponce)

Two remote, chromatic chords form a beautiful final cadence that sounds as inevitable as it is unusual. The bass line moves up chromatically and the last chord is approached by contrary, chromatic motion.

CHORDS OF THE SIXTH

The flattened supertonic is the site of the first chord with a 'geographical' name that we shall meet. The major triad on this site, in its first inversion, is called the **Neapolitan sixth** – the interval between its lowest and highest notes – e.g. F A♭ D♭ in the key of C: why 'Neapolitan' no one now knows. It may be found in various situations, most often followed by dominant or tonic harmony:

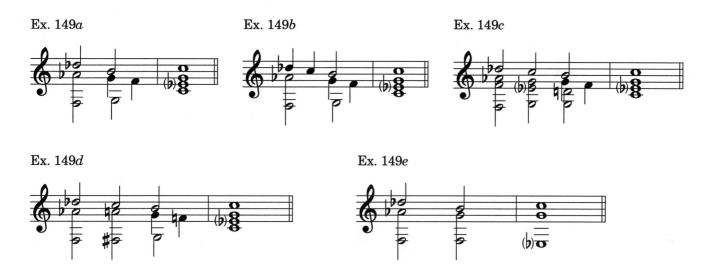

Ex. 149a Ex. 149b Ex. 149c

Ex. 149d Ex. 149e

The chord is also considered by some to be the triad on the supertonic, with both root and fifth lowered: a somewhat devious explanation, but perhaps more plausible if Ex. 149 is replayed, omitting the flats on each D and A, to give a clear relationship to ii♭ in each case. The cadence ♭II♭ – V(7)ₐ in the forms shown in Exs. 149a and b is often called the **pathetic cadence** on account of its air of pathos; it is slightly weakened by the passing note in b, but even more so by the intervening chords in c and d. Instances of the Neapolitan sixth in guitar music are shown in Ex. 150.

Ex. 150a (Sor)

Ex. 150b (Tansman)

Ex. 150c (Sor)

Ex. 150*d* (Tárrega)

Ex. 150*e* (Tárrega)

Ex. 150*f* (Duarte)

Ex. 150*g* (Carcassi)

150*h* (Bach)

a)   A 'pathetic' cadence of type *b* above, the chords presented as arpeggios.

b)   Similar to *a* but: (1) the resolution is of type *e* above, and (2) the D♯ at the end of the first complete bar, a chromatic passing note, foreshadows the resolution.

c)   The resolution is of type *c* above, the chords again arpeggiated.

d)   The Neapolitan sixth first appears in its usual position and is then arpeggiated as from the 'root position'. Resolution is arbitrary but effective, the parts not moving by step.

e)   The preceding passage is in D major, in which key this 'vamp till ready' bar continues. In the next it changes to the tonic minor key, and a Neapolitan sixth is used, in 'root position' and not its usual first inversion, to anticipate the greater pathos.

f) g) These are unusual ways of quitting the Neapolitan sixth, the more usual resolution merely delayed in each case.

h) The prevailing key is B minor; the chord of G (VI) is a nexus, assuming the role of a Neapolitan sixth and hinging on the dominant of F♯ minor, the resolution being of type *e* above. As in example *e* of this group, the chord is in 'root position', as defined by its lowest note; however, if the bass B at the beginning of the bar is considered to be retained in the memory it puts the chord in its standard position.

CHORDS OF THE AUGMENTED SIXTH

These form an important group of chromatic chords, also with geographical names that are not now explicable. Like the Neapolitan sixth they may, in theory, be built on *any* degree of the scale but, in practice, they are usually based on only a limited number of sites. Their derivation may most easily be seen as in Ex. 151 where they are formed on the flattened supertonic of C, one note of the first chord being doubled at the octave though, of course, it is not necessary for it to be so in normal use. This succession is easily remembered by the mnemonic *'I For-Get'*, for Italian, French, German.

Ex. 151

Italian   French   German

In their close position they are bounded by an augmented sixth, hence their family name. They are both colourful and extremely useful, facts of which composers have been aware for more than 250 years, and not least during the nineteenth century when such harmonies were valued for their effect.

The boundary interval usually resolves by expansion (leaning note plus leading note) to an octave, normally the root of the next chord:

Ex. 152

Ex. 153*a* (Sor)

Ex. 153*b* (Giuliani)

Ex. 153c (Carcassi)

Ex. 153d (Giuliani)

Ex. 153e (Duarte)

Ex. 153f (idem)

Ex. 153g (Castelnuovo-Tedesco)

Ex. 153h (Carcassi)

Ex. 153i (Castelnuovo-Tedesco)

Ex. 153j (Giuliani)

Ex. 153k (Tórroba)

Ex. 153*l* (Sor)

Ex. 153*m* (Ponce)

The augmented sixths are usually found, as in Ex. 151, on either the flattened supertonic or submediant, resolving as 'quasi' dominant or dominant-of-dominant chords; exceptions occur, some of which are among the passages quoted in Ex. 153:

a)   Italian sixth on the submediant (which is already lowered in the harmonic minor scale), growing naturally out of iv_b (key is B minor) and leading to V_a.

b)   Italian sixth on the submediant (key is D minor) resulting from the contrary, chromatic movement of treble and bass lines.

c)   Italian sixth on the flattened submediant, smoothly following IV_b and resolving on to tonic six-four.

d)   Italian sixth on the flattened submediant, preceded by vi_a and resolving on to tonic six-four, as also in c albeit incomplete.

e)   Incomplete French sixth on the flattened supertonic (missing note is A); the resumption after the pause does not represent a formal resolution.

f)   Incomplete French sixth on the flattened submediant (missing note is again A), resolving on to tonic harmony.

g)   German sixth on the flattened supertonic (end of bar 1) resolving on to I_a. After one bar, in which the dominant seventh of a new key is introduced, a French sixth appears (bar 3) on the new flattened supertonic, in turn resolving on to the new i_a.

h)   French sixth on the flattened submediant, inverted and resolving on to $V7_a$.

i)   German sixth on the flattened dominant, inverted and resolving on to iv_a and thence on to tonic six-four.

j)   German sixth on the flattened submediant, resolving on to tonic six-four.

k)   Incomplete German sixth on the flattened submediant, resolving on to V7$_a$. The E♭ should be read as D♯.

l)   The moving inner part creates a succession of augmented-sixth chords in the order: Italian/German/French/Italian/French/German. The key of the moment is D major and the sixths are thus based on the flattened supertonic, the last resolving on to I$_a$. This device was much used in the period of this piece and numerous other examples, especially by Sor, may be found.

m)   The third bar has suggestions of all three augmented sixths: French (*first* note plus chord, cumulative effect); Italian (chord alone); and German (chord plus last note, cumulative). All three are based on the subdominant and resolve on to the mediant major triad (C); no change of key takes place and, in the next bar, the music resumes without ceremony in the original key of A♭.

Chromatic harmony may result from the chromatic movement of one or more voices. The resulting chords may be analysed, but this is not always important; a passage may be carried along on the tide of the chromatic flow, creating its own 'logic'. In Ex. 154 a chromatic bass line ascends beneath a diatonic melody that suggests pealing bells. Ex. 154*a* has the two lines set simply against one another; in *b* the chromatic line is extended to thirds and in *c* to sixths, with some accommodating adjustments to bar 2.

Ex. 154*a* (Castelnuovo-Tedesco)

Ex. 154*b*

Ex. 154*c*

Further examples of such chromaticism are given in Ex. 155:

Ex. 155*a* (Dowland)

a) The piece is based on a descending, chromatic sequence of six notes; its three overlapping appearances are marked by asterisks. Other, incomplete entries may be found, for example the second entry begins with the B in the middle voice and, at the same point, another starts with the G below it, but continues for only five notes, to D♯.

Ex.155*b (ibid.)*

b) Three overlapping entries, the second beginning with the asterisked E at the end of bar 1.

Ex. 155*c* (Dowland)

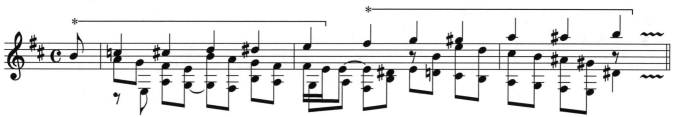

c) This fantasia, based on a *rising* chromatic hexachord, mirrors the other. Two successive entries in the highest voice are set against *descending* and largely diatonic movement.

Ex. 155*d (ibid.)*

d) Four overlapping entries begin at the asterisked points.

Ex. 155*e* (Castelnuovo-Tedesco)

e) A lullaby: the melody is diatonic, the bass remains soporifically fixed, the middle voice climbs steadily and chromatically.

f)   The melody, built on a modal scale (see Ex. 12*g*, p. 20), rises; the bass line treads chromatically downward, with an enforced octave leap between the last two bars.

Ex. 155*g* *(idem)*

g)   The offset, downward movement (mostly chromatic) of the two upper parts produces a succession of strong dissonances.

Remote Modulation

The possibilities of remote modulation are innumerable and beyond the scope of this book to discuss systematically. Key changes, since the classical period, have tended to be transitions rather than modulations, less time being devoted to the formality of erasing one key and introducing another.

Ex. 156*a* (Giuliani)

A pivot transition in which the note E, dominant of A major, becomes the mediant of C major (the passage is paraphrased to its essential harmony). The change is from a major key to the major on the flattened mediant (A to C).

Ex. 156*b* (Ponce)

A transition via a deceptive cadence. V^7 of C major is followed by the expected melody note, C, but supported by the chord of the flattened sub-mediant (major), quickly established over a tonic pedal by its own dominant, a shift from C major to A♭ major.

Ex. 156*c* (Castelnuovo-Tedesco)

A pivot transition involving an enharmonic change: B♭, dominant of E♭, becomes A♯, the mediant of the second (F♯), a shift from a major key to the raised supertonic major (E♭ to F♯).

Ex. 156*d* (Duarte)

The home key is E major; the music hesitates on the V^7 before continuing with a chord that might be either iii^7 in C major or a 'modal' seventh in A minor; the true key does not declare itself, but it is at least 'four degrees flatter'.

Ex. 156*e* (Tárrega)

The diminished seventh chord (asterisked) acts as a nexus, sharing two notes with the tonic triad of the first key (A minor) and three with the V^7 of the second one's V^7 (the dominant of its dominant) if C = B♯. The move is thus from A minor to F♯ major, a very remote one.

Ex. 156*f* (Pujol)

The music, in A major, turns abruptly to the tonic minor (A minor), whose VI, asterisked, acts as a simple nexus leading to B♭ major, the flattened supertonic key.

Ex. 156*g* (Ponce)

The downward scale of the home key stops on the subdominant (B♭) which acts as a pivot note, becoming the mediant of the new key (G♭ major); again, a transition to the flattened supertonic key via a different route.

Ex. 156*h* (Ponce)

The first quotation shows the opening of the movement, the second occurs later. C♯ is the nexus on which transition is made: the leading note of the home key becomes the tonic of the new – minor to leading-note minor.

Ex. 156*i* (Duarte)

The pivot note is D, tonic of the home key (D minor) and mediant of the new (B minor); the process is, as with *b*, akin to an interrupted cadence.

Ex. 156*j* (Duarte)

From the prevailing key of B minor there is a transition to that of G minor. The original mediant note (D) becomes the new dominant.

These few examples give some indication of the variety of means for making transitions – which are the most common form of key-change in guitar music – in keeping with both modern musical trends and with the comparative brevity of guitar music itself. Those interested in the longer and more leisurely process of modulation will find a good example in Sor's Sonata, Op. 25, in the passage involving the turn from page 11 to 12 (Ricordi edition BA. 9600), a progressive shift from C major to A♭ major (compare and contrast Ex. 156*b*).

Pedal Points

A pedal point, briefly mentioned on p. 80, occurs when a constant (pedal) note is maintained while the rest of the harmony changes, often producing harsh dissonances. Whether the effect originated, as is sometimes said, with an organist who left his foot on one pedal for too long is not known. The pedal note itself may be the lowest voice in the passage (a genuine 'pedal') or the highest ('inverted pedal') or a middle voice ('internal pedal'). Most frequently the pedal note is the tonic or the dominant of the prevailing key.

According to context and content, pedal points may have different emotional effects. If the mood is quiet and/or pastoral, with no really 'acidic' disagreement between the pedal note and the remainder, the effect is soothing or hypnotic, the pedal note acting as a steadying influence. Under livelier circumstances it may generate a feeling ranging from mild expectancy to taut tension, a need to be released from the mounting dissonance. Guitar music abounds in examples of pedal points, many owed to the convenience of using an open string as the pedal note. Ex. 157 gives some of these.

Ex. 157a (Sor)

Ex. 157b (Castelnuovo-Tedesco)

Ex. 157c (Duarte)

Ex. 157d (Traditional Catalan, arr. Llobet)

Ex. 157e (Tórroba)

134

Ex. 157*f* (Duarte)

Ex. 157*g* (Dodgson)

Ex. 157*h* (Bach)

Ex. 157*i* (Sor)

Ex.157*j* (Sor)

Ex. 157*k* (*ibid*)

Ex. 157*l* (Duarte)

TONIC PEDALS

a)   A rather static effect with which one expects the music to break free from the simple assertion of the key (cf. Exs. 99*a* and *b*).

b)   and (*c*) Two lullabies, each using a rocking ostinato figure, both containing only diatonic notes and producing a soothing effect.

d)   Skeletal I, IV and V give a gentle increase in tension before release to the tonic (again cf. *a*).

e)   Despite fairly strong clashes the air is calm and tension is released when, with the asterisked chord, V7-9 is reached.

f)   The internal pedal note (E) enhances the vigour of the music.

g)   The melodic line hops from one side of the pedal (A) to the other; as the passage proceeds it becomes more dissonant.

h)   Dissonance increases as the pedal point continues. Pedal points are common features in fugues.

DOMINANT PEDALS

i)   An internal pedal that never disagrees with its surroundings; the ebb and flow of tension depends on the identity and inversion of each diatonic chord produced in passing. The opening bars of Tárrega's 'Lagrima' provide a similar example.

j)   Surprisingly, the opening of the piece, but lacking real tension.

k)   The later appearance of the same passage as *j* develops a little more tension with its chromatic intrusions, but discards the pedal and adopts a relaxed harmonization.

l)   The pedal point increases its tension: (i) by ascending pitch, (ii) by increasing use of shorter notes (quavers), and (iii) through growing disagreement between the pedal note and the keys implied by the upper parts. It then unwinds by descending in pitch to a triumphant return of tonic harmony. The fugue with which Ponce's 'Folias Variations' ends has, on its last page (Schott GA 135) a similar pedal point, longer, and unwinding by reversing all three processes (i)–(iii).

Open first and sixth strings provide a persistent tonic pedal throughout Villa-Lobos' Study No. 1, while in the present author's Toccata Op. 18 (Broekmans and van Poppel No. 936) the open fifth string provides a tonic pedal and the first a simultaneous dominant one, changing in the middle section to the open sixth and second strings, which do likewise in the new key.

Steps Beyond

In past centuries music followed a course of evolution that is in retrospect remarkably orderly and even 'predictable'; in the 20th century it, together with most other areas of human activity, positively 'exploded'. The very rate of progress has itself created problems in coming to terms with a rapid succession of radically new concepts, many asking for the acceptance of what would not before have been regarded as music, good or bad. This has been exacerbated by the fact that composers no longer speak variants of the same identifiable language but now pursue vastly different aesthetic objectives, often creating their own musical processes in doing so. There is no longer one line of development and the listener or analyst is frequently left to find for him/herself what the composer is trying to express, and through what means. Never before has the *avant-garde* been so far out of touch with the ordinary listening public, and even with many professional musicians, and the gap widens as the pace of events increases beyond our normal capacity to absorb and understand; often we are invited or, rather, told that it is necessary to 'wipe our ears clean' and to discard our established listening habits, which is much more easily said than done. For most people salvation lies in listening and trying to decide subjectively what the new music 'says', if anything, even though they may not even faintly understand the grammar and syntax of its language.

To attempt an orderly and comprehensive account of 20th century musical evolution would be to double the size of this book, and this would not be justifiable. First, the guitar has yet to penetrate many areas of contemporary music and has entered others to a very limited extent. It would thus be impossible to illustrate every point by reference to guitar music. Second, and equally important, it is perhaps too soon to attempt to do for today's music what Prout and his successors have done for that of earlier times. While many excellent and exhaustive textbooks exist for what we may term 'conventional' music, there are very few indeed that approach this status with contemporary music; most are discursive rather than detailed, and others deal with specific areas of development only. Textbooks have always followed practice at a respectful distance, becoming viable only when the dust has settled and significant trends have become established by long-term survival. History has its own way of rejecting the unimportant, all too often rejecting assessments made at the time particular music was written. In the early nineteenth century, an age of more leisurely progress and much less diversity than our own, Beethoven was considered by many responsible musicians to be a madman, whereas Diabelli was highly regarded. While to us this may seem incredible, we may rightly wonder how our own contemporary music will be evaluated in 100 or even 50 years' time. The remainder of this book therefore makes no pretence to comprehensiveness. Readers interested in pursuing the matter of twentieth-century musical practice are recommended to consult the general literature, in particular: *The New Music* by Reginald Smith-Brindle (Oxford), *Tonality, Atonality and Pantonality* by Rudolph Reti (Rockliff) and *Boulez on Music Today* (Faber).

CHORDS BUILT WITH DIFFERENT INTERVALS

Traditional harmony is solidly based, as we have seen, on the use of the triads and their extensions. Some composers, feeling this vein to have been exhausted, have constructed chords by replacing thirds with other intervals, of which the most favoured has been the fourth. Such chords are treated in their own right and not, even in a purely diatonic context, regarded as necessary to resolve, though they often sound quite dissonant. At a time when our notions of consonance and dissonance (which have always been relative and not absolute are very flexible, this is not difficult to accept. Guitar composers have embraced this device, which fits neatly with the tuning of the instrument – a simple barré can produce chords composed either wholly or partially of fourths. Ex. 158 shows a few examples, of which the first arpeggiates its chords as overtly as any nineteenth-century study by Carcassi or Sor. Chords composed of piled fourths will, on inversion and/or redistribution, automatically contain seconds and fifths, as in the last example, Ex. 158*h*.

Ex. 158*a* (Duarte)

Ex. 158*b* *(idem)*

Ex. 158*c* (Duarte)

Ex. 158*d* (Castelnuovo-Tedesco)

Ex. 158*e* (Castelnuovo-Tedesco)

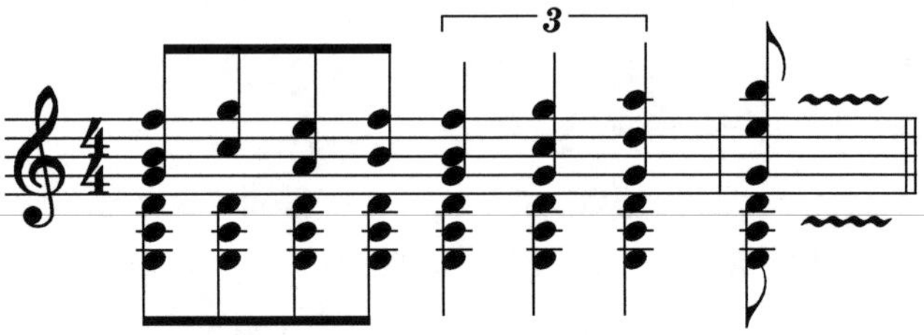

Ex. 158*f* (De Filippi)

Ex. 158*g* (Cammarota)

Ex. 158h (Wills)

Chords have also been formed from seconds, again treated as though requiring no resolution despite their dissonance; they are referred to as **clusters**. For technical reasons they are not common in guitar music and most often require one open string to make them practicable; with two or more guitars there is no difficulty – the second movement of the present author's 'Going Dutch', Op. 36, for four guitars (Broekmans & van Poppel 868) contains a passage in clusters, evoking the sounds of bells. Some examples are shown in Ex. 159. In *a* the passage recalls the ability of the baroque guitar, with its re-entrant tuning, to allow the notes of a scale to chime together, producing a cumulative chord – the *campanile* effect. The second and third present the clusters as 'arpeggios', in the latter case assisted by the use of ligados that make the clusters sound more dense than they in fact are. A simple method of producing a cluster is of course to sit on a piano keyboard!

Ex. 159a (Duarte)

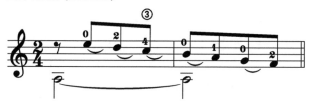

Ex. 159b *(idem)*

Ex. 159c (Brouwer)

GRATUITOUS DISSONANCES

Familiar chords, e.g. I, IV, and V, are sometimes used with additional notes that create acid dissonances for their own sake, introduced to produce a wry or sardonic effect, as in Ex. 160, where in *b* the passage is rewritten without its added spicing of dissonance.

Ex. 160*a* (Duarte)

Ex. 160*b*

This usage is common in the music of Joaquin Rodrigo, for example in the *Fandango* and the *Concierto de Aranjuez*.

THE UNDERMINING OF TONALITY

From the earliest recorded times music has retained the broad concept of *tonality*, the acknowledgement of the central importance of one note (the tonic, final, or key-note) and the organization of other notes in relation to it. Even the use of the modes, albeit non-harmonic, revolves around this principle. The later concept of 'key' did likewise, reinforcing it with harmony that 'pointed in the right directions'. Tonality became a broader concept, embracing relationships with other keys, at first those of the close family of V, IV, vi, iii, and ii, and later widening it until, in the nineteenth century, all others fell within its scope. Many 20th century practices have, to varying extents, contributed to the weakening of the effect of the tonic, an undermining of 'parental authority' that has had social and political counterparts. Some of the approaches listed below have only a mild effect, but they nevertheless reflect the move away from clear-cut methods of establishing firm tonality, or even key.

The four examples of Ex. 161 obscure tonality in varying degree, simply by the use of triads. The bass-line of *a* alone keeps the music oriented toward A. In *d* the music consistently oscillates between subdominant major and minor harmony and at the end (the bars shown) leaves us in the inconclusive, dreamlike state proper to a *berceuse*.

Ex. 161*a* (Rosetta)

Ex.161*b* (Haug)

Ex. 161c (Wissmer)

Ex. 161d (Tansman)

Ex. 161a also exemplifies another free usage in harmony; for most of its length the three-note chords are minor triads, in root position and close spacing, that is, the same chord moved up and down in parallel. This practice has been widely used by composers for the guitar and, though it has been compared to organum (p. 49) – a resemblance that is at best superficial – it amounts to the 'coloration' of each melody note with the same hue, the application of a chord for the sake of its colour rather than the logic of its placing; as though an artist chose to paint the features of a human face in shades of the same blue (as has been done) though this is in a sense against nature and illogical. The obvious attraction of the method in our context is that it is easy to shift a constant fingerboard pattern up and down and, for a non-playing composer, a safe assumption that it is so. Since each chord differs from its companion in pitch-level only, and thus does not necessarily have a strongly directional effect, there is little or no disturbance of the feeling of tonality, and the course of the melodic line is not deflected; the chords simply add a pleasant harmonic colour to each note.

Ex. 162a (Castelnuovo-Tedesco)

An example of 'marking time'. The first chord, I in the home key, launches a brief chromatic excursion that returns, immediately following the passage quoted, to the same place.

Ex. 162b (Castelnuovo-Tedesco)

A pedal note maintains the feeling of tonality.

Ex. 162c (Villa-Lobos)

In the context, and over a tonic pedal, the parallel chords of the ninth (minus their roots) add interest but do not impair the sense of tonality.

Ex. 162*d (idem)*

A similar passage, over a dominant pedal, has dominant seventh chords similarly used, the open B string acting as an internal pedal and creating passing dissonances, but with only coloristic effect.

Ex. 162*e* (Villa-Lobos)

Parallel major triads move against an inverted pedal formed by the open E and B strings, the total effect having something of the flavour of flamenco. This is characteristic of Villa-Lobos' writing.

The foregoing processes blur tonality to different extents but do not destroy it. A more potent method is to *multiply* it, to introduce a real degree of loyalty to more than one tonic at once.

Ex. 163*a* (Duarte)

The upper line is a simple ostinato pointing to a tonic of E, the lower is clearly in A♭ major.

Ex. 163*b* (Duarte)

The upper line is firmly in E♭ minor, the lower points in A minor, while in Ex. 163*c*

Ex. 163c (*ibid*)

the middle voice is in G major and the outer ones are consistent with the remote key of D♭ major.

Such passages are said to exhibit **bitonality**, the simultaneous use of two keys.

Ex. 163d (Duarte)

Two keys are admixed in each single line (A minor and B♭ major), with some mild clashes produced by the canon (or, since it is from a fugue, a *stretto*).

When more than two keys are used at the same time the result is **polytonality**, a situation that is difficult, for technical reasons, to bring to the guitar. The juxtaposition of different keys may however be more kaleidoscopic and fleeting, with shifting allegiances to numerous tonics or suggestions of unrelated keys that are not clearly defined. This situation is termed **pantonality** and, in different forms, is the language of much contemporary guitar music. A step in this direction is exemplified in Ex. 164a where the lower part remains for six bars in C major, sliding in bar 7 toward a flatter key, while the upper one suggests a succession of remote keys – possibly E♭, A, D♭ and G majors – but does not define them precisely.

Ex. 164a (Duarte)

Later in the work from which Exs. 163b and c are taken, the four keys are drawn together in the form of their tonic triads, arpeggiated (D♭ appears as C♯), in the form of a canon. Though four keys are indicated, only two occur at any one moment; the effect is thus of shifting bitonality.

Ex. 164b (Duarte)

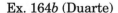

Exs. l64c, d and e are all taken from the same work (Britten's 'Nocturnal', Op. 70). In c the open strings provide a pedal of 'white notes' only; the outer parts (doubling one another at the double octave) hint at a key of at least three flats. In the course of the movement the outer parts traverse a variety of remote keys, for the most part not clearly defined. The chords of d provide a V-I close in A major, but the melody, at first consistent with F major, ends inconclusively, suggesting E♭ minor. The passage in e is even more kaleidoscopic, the lower (*ostinato*) line is rooted in C major (or A minor) but the upper runs through G minor, A major and E minor in quick succession, defining them with fair clarity.

Ex. 164c (Britten)

Ex. 164d *(idem)*

Ex. 164e *(idem)*

The whole work abounds in examples of mixed tonality; though it reaches, with Dowland's music, the key of E major at its end, it dissolves inconclusively into 'ambiguous silence'.

The area of mixed tonality is a very large one, and it does not always follow that a composer employs any one form of it throughout a work. Tom Eastwood's 'Ballade-Phantasy' (Faber) contains many passages of mixed tonality and others that are clearly tonal.

THE NEGATION OF TONALITY

The varied methods used in the 20th century to obscure tonality sprang from the feeling of some composers that the established tonal language was exhausted – a premise on which events have since cast some doubt. A step beyond the clouding of tonality is to destroy it – the King is dead, long live the commune. Though it has had a tremendous impact on music, this approach has not become the mainstream of progress (nor, for that matter, has any other): in its most rigid form it has been virtually abandoned. In different ways it has been absorbed into the total language of music as an additional resource. For a full and remarkably lucid account of a vast subject, the reader should refer to *Serial Composition* by Reginald Smith Brindle (Oxford). It can be dealt with here only sufficiently to give an indication of the principles involved.

To negate tonality and to establish **atonality** (a state of no tonality) it is necessary to avoid the chance of any one note assuming, however briefly, the role of tonic; this is most usually done by observing certain guiding principles. It must be stressed that composers have always exercised their right to modify these 'rules' by the use of their imagination and discretion.

i) The raw material from which the work is constructed is the **note row** (American: **tone row**), in which the twelve different notes (the twelve semitones within an octave) are arranged in an order decided by the composer. Composition begins with the formulation of the note row.

ii) In the strictest practice no three successive notes may form a triad and, therefore, imply a tonic chord.

iii) The notes of the row are used, in order of appearance, to form either lines of 'melody' or chords. In practice the order is frequently changed and notes omitted.

iv) No one note should be re-used (reiterations do not count) until all the others have been used; equal rights are the objective. Again, composers have used their discretion.

v) The row may be subjected to various modifications, all of which may be used in the above ways:

a) Inversion: each interval step in the original row (O) is reversed, *not* inverted in the 'tonal' sense we have learned. For instance, if a row begins by ascending through C, D and A♭, its inversion begins by descending through C, B♭, and E.

b) Retrograde: the order of the notes is reversed, i.e. 1–12 becomes 12–1.

c) Retrograde inversion: backwards *and* upside down.

d) Transposed: the row, in any of its forms (O, I, R, RI) transposed to begin at any other pitch.

e) Derivatives may be devised by systematic alteration of the order of the notes. For example:

1	2	3	4	5	6	7	8	9	10	11	12	
1	3	5	7	9	11	2	4	6	8	10	12	(alternate notes)
1	4	7	10	2	5	8	11	3	6	9	12	(every third note)

Any of these may be modified in any of the ways listed in *(a)–(d)*.

vi) It is not necessary to preserve the profile of the original row, nor to place any note in the same octave as in its first statement. Separation by wide intervals is frequent, since this weakens any impression of tonal relationship between successive or simultaneous notes.

vii) Since the traditional relationships between notes do not apply, any note may be 'spelled' in any way, at any time: i.e. any enharmonic notation may be used.

Writing along the foregoing lines is termed **serial composition**, for obvious reasons. All atonal music is not necessarily serial, but all serial writing in accordance with the guidelines is essentially atonal. The term *twelve note*, (American 'twelve-tone') and its Greek form '**dodecaphonic**' are often freely, if not always accurately, used to describe atonal or serial music. In **total serialization** note durations are also controlled by the same means as pitch, to avoid possible implications of cadence or phrasing inherent in familiar rhythmic patterns. As it too often leads to a score that defies accurate performance, total serialization is not now widely used. This is true also of strict serial writing in general, and a 'counter-revolution' against the dictatorship of mathematics (even when mollified by a composer's discretion) has led many writers to use 'impure' forms of atonality (serial or not) and even to mix atonality with tonality. Atonality is now the 'twenty-fifth tonality' – twelve major, twelve minor, one 'neutral' – an additional compositional resource.

Ex. 165*a* (Duarte)

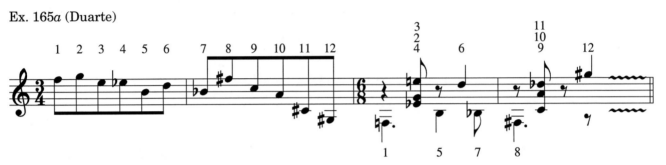

The row is first stated alone and then 'fragmented'.

Ex. 165*b* *(idem)*

Ex.165*b* gives the end of the movement of which *a* is the beginning: distinct elements of tonality do not give any feeling of the establishment of one key, even though the final chord is in effect a second inversion of C♯ major.

Ex. 165*c* (Norman)

Once stated, the row is treated very freely with respect to note-order.

Ex. 165*d* (Fink)

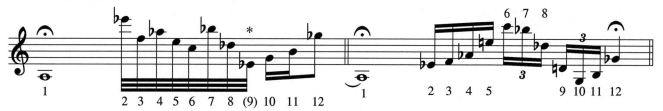

In Ex.165*d* the row is given twice, in order, but with different profiles. The asterisked note is probably an error.

Ex. 165*e* (Santorsola)   Inversion

Ex. 165*f* (ibid)

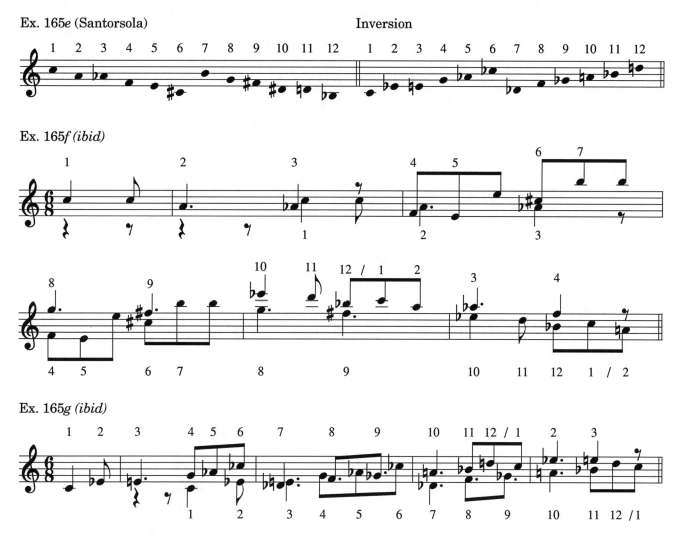

In Exs. 165*e-k* the composer declares his note row at the head of each movement. That of the first is given in *e*, both original and inverted. In *f* it is used to form a canon in which the parts cross in the first two bars. Ex. 165*g* is a canon formed from the inversion, again with part-crossing in the second bar.

Ex. 165*h* (ibid)

Ex. 165*i* *(ibid)*

Ex. 165*j* *(ibid)*

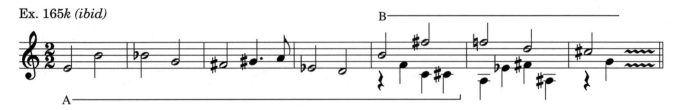

The row of the second movement (*h*) is divided into two-note chords (*i*) and then into four successive notes and two four-note chords; the numerical manipulation is clear. Ex. 165*j* uses the retrograde form, freely, to form a two-step sequence.

Ex. 165*k* *(ibid)*

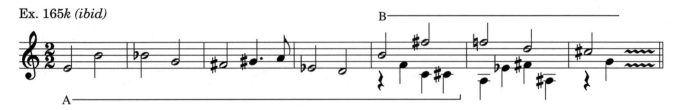

Ex. 165*k* is from the finale of the same work: the row (from A) is transposed (from B) upwards, by a perfect fifth.

A simple example of derivative rows is provided by the second movement of Fernando Sulpizi's *Falene* (Bèrben 2147), which proceeds throughout in notes of equal length. After a statement of the note row a chord appears, consisting (bass to treble) of 1 3 2 6 5 4, the first six notes in an order largely dictated by the guitar itself; recurrences of this chord, complete or incomplete, divide the music into sections within which the note-order is as follows:

1.	1		2	3	4	5	6		(chord notes, in numerical order)
		7	8	9	10	11	12		(others, also in order)
2.	1	3	2	6	5	4			(chord notes, in bass-to-treble order)
		7	8	9	10	11	12		(others, in order)
3.	1	3	2	6	5	4			(chord notes, in bass-to-treble order)
	12	11	10	9	8	7			(others, in retrograde order)
4.	1	3	2	6	5	4			(chord notes, as in 2. and 3.)
	12	11	10	7	8	9			(others: first three retrograde, last three normal)
5.	As 2.								
6.	4	5	6	2	3	1			(chord notes, bass-to-treble, in retrograde order)
		7	8	9	10	11	12		(others, in order)
7.	2	3	1						(first three chord notes in retrograde order)
		7	8						(others, first two only, in normal order)

Elizabeth Lutyens' 'The Dying of the Sun' (published by the composer), though freely atonal in language, begins and ends with the same note, ironically a trait of tonal music. The music however conveys no impression of allegiance to this note (A, the first of the row), but rather of departure from and return to a state of 'nothing', the rising and setting of the sun, to which a programmatic note gives deeper significance. Half-way through, the twelfth note (G) is repeated and the music returns, in reverse, to its beginning; the halves are thus in effect mirror-images of one another.

The atonal language in music has passed its apogee and has become a part of the whole, but atonal works for the guitar are still far from plentiful, and most guitarists remain content to share the conservatism of their audiences by not playing those that there are. The *Suite* by Krenek (Doblinger 05906) is almost alone in receiving even sporadic performances.

Other directions taken by music in our time include:
(i)   the exploitation of instruments for every kind of sound they can produce, pitched and otherwise;
(ii)   the absorption of 'non-musical' sounds other than those of percussion instruments;
(iii) composition by chance (**aleatory**) means, the content and/or its order of perfonnance being decided by such processes as throwing dice;
(iv)   directives to performers to improvise, either by manipulating a given musical working-stock or unit, or by choosing their own notes together with their durations and dynamics. A work may consist wholly or partially of such activity, and improvisation may be invited with defined musical material, or in response to graphical scores, pictorial designs, or whimsical drawings;
(v)   electronically produced sounds, generated by synthesizers and organized by heavily mathematical procedures;
(vi)   the preparation of tapes containing assembled, 'processed' sounds of various origins, and in some instances playing 'in duo' with such tapes.

There now seems to be little that is not regarded, by *someone*, as music; John Cage even benefits from royalties resulting from his directive to performers to sit in silence for a precise length of time. In all this the guitar has had little part, and any extended account of it here would not be justified. Much of it is also debatable as 'composition', with so much responsibility for content being passed to the performer and with inevitable and radical differences between one performance of a work and the next. At all events it is a field in flux, and barely susceptible to the type of treatment followed by this book. Whether or not guitarists become a meaningful part of these progressive areas is something we must wait to find out.

APPENDIX I

Music Quoted In Examples In Text

Numbers on the extreme right identify the examples in the text (see Appendix II). Publishers' references are given except:

    i) where the item is common and available in several good editions.

    ii) where the example has been adapted by the author from the original music, and no guitar edition is known.

    iii) with items arranged from lute and other tablatures, and for which no guitar edition is known.

Music merely referred to in the course of the text but not quoted in staff notation is not included in this list.

ABSIL, JEAN:
    Le Petit Bestiaire (Bèrben 1711) La Poule — 1a
    Romance (Bèrben 1871) — 1b

AGUADO, DIONYSIO:
    Study No. 16 (Schott GA 62) — 2

ANONYMOUS:
    Gigue (Universal 13942) — 3a
    Heaven and Earth, from Sampson Lute-book (Zanibon 5579) — 3b

BACH, J.S.:
    Song: *Bist du bei mir* from *Anna-Magdalena Büchlein* — 4
    Cello Suite No. 1, BWV 1007 (Schott GA 213) Prelude — 5
    Cello Suite No. 3, BWV 1009 (Schott GA 214) Allemande — 6a
    Cello Suite No. 3, BWV 1009 (Schott GA 214) Bourrée — 6b
    Cello Suite No. 3, BWV 1009 (Schott GA 214) Prelude — 6c
    Mass in B minor, BWV 232, *Agnus Dei* — 7
    Lute Suite No. 1, BWV 996, Bourrée — 8
    Lute Suite No. 2, BWV 995, Double — 9a
    Lute Suite No. 2, BWV 995, Prelude — 9b
    Lute Suite No. 3, BWV 997, Prelude — 10
    Lute Suite No. 4, BWV 1006a, Menuet — 11
    Partita No. 5, BWV 829, Minuet (Schott 11081) — 12
    Prelude, BWV 999 (in D minor for guitar) — 13
    Prelude, Fugue and Allegro, BWV 998, Fugue — 14a
    Prelude, Fugue and Allegro, BWV 998, Prelude — 14b
    Two-part Invention No. 4, BWV 775 — 15
    Violin Partita No. 1, BWV 1002, Bourrée — 16a
    Violin Partita No. 1, BWV 1002, Sarabande — 16b
    Violin Partita No. 2, BWV 1004, Chaconne — 17
    Violin Sonata No. 1, BWV 1001, Fugue (in A minor for guitar) — 18
    Well-tempered Clavier, Book I, Prelude No. 1, BWV 846 — 19a
    Well-tempered Clavier, Book I, Prelude No. 8, BWV 853 — 19b

BADINGS, HENK:
    12 Preludes (Bèrben 1641) No. 1 — 20

BARFARK, BALINT (Valentin):
    Ricercare I, 1553 — 21
    Ricercate, 1553 — 22

BATCHELAR, DANIEL:
    Mounsiers Almaine (Bèrben 1592) — 23

BEETHOVEN, LUDWIG VAN:
    Sonata, Op. 14/2 (Novello) Andante — 24
    Symphony No. 5, 2nd movement — 25
    Violin Concerto, 2nd movement — 26

BERKELEY, SIR LENNOX:
    Theme and Variations (Bèrben 1643) — 27

BLYTON, CARY:
    In Memoriam Django Reinhardt (Bèrben 1712) — 28

BRITTEN, (LORD) BENJAMIN:
    Nocturnal, Op. 70 (Faber) — 29

BROUWER, LEO:
    La Espiral Eterna (Schott GA 423) — 30

BURKHART, FRANZ:
    Passacaglia (Universal 11959) — 31

CAMMAROTA, CARLO:
    Acquarelli Napoletani (Zanibon 5262) Notturno — 32

CAPIROLA, VINCENZO:
    Padoana alla Francese (Universal 29155) — 33

CARCASSI, MATTEO:
    Allegretto, Op. 21/17 — 34
    Op. 4/2 — 35
    Study, Op. 60/3 — 36
    Study, Op. 60/8 — 37
    Study, Op. 60/19 — 38

CARULLI, FERDINANDO:
    Allegretto — 39
    Andante — 40
    Rondo — 41
    Study in A minor — 42
    Variations, Op. 142 — 43

CASTELNUOVO-TEDESCO, MARIO:
    Appunti, Op. 210 (Suvini Zerboni 6725) No. 8 — 44a
    Appunti, Op. 210 (Suvini Zerboni 6854) Minuetto — 44b
    Platero y Yo (Bèrben 1701) Primavera — 45a
    Platero y Yo (Bèrben 1703) La Arrulladora — 45b
    Platero y Yo (Bèrben 1703) The Canary Dies — 45c
    Platero y Yo (Bèrben 1703) La Muerte — 45d
    Platero y Yo (Bèrben 1704) Domingo — 45e
    Platero y Yo (Bèrben 1704) La Flor del Camino — 45f
    Platero y Yo (Bèrben 1704) Golondriñas — 45g
    Platero y Yo (Bèrben 1704) Los Gitanos — 45g
    Platero y Yo (Bèrben 1704) Convalescence — 45h
    Sonata 'Homage to Boccherini' (Schott GA 149) 1st movement — 46

COLLARD, EDWARD:
    Galliard (Universal 29160) — 47

COSTE, NAPOLEON:
    Valse, Op. 41/8 (Schott GA 12) — 48

COUPERIN, FRANÇOIS:
    Les Barricades Mystérieuses (Bèrben 1844) — 49

COUPERIN, LOUIS:
    Chaconne, Bauyn 122 (Novello) — 50
    La Piemontaise, Bauyn 103 (Novello) — 51
    Sarabande, Bauyn 96 (Novello) — 52

CREMA, JOAN, MARIA DA:
 Ricercare (Bèrben 2122) No. IV 53
 Ricercare (Bèrben 2122) No. IX 54
CUTTING, FRANCIS:
 Galliard (Oxford 19.356001.1) 55
DIABELLI, ANTON:
 Viennese Waltz (Universal 14463) 56
DLUGORAJ, ALBERT:
 Fantasia, 1603 57
DODGSON, STEPHEN:
 Partita (Oxford) 58
DOWLAND, JOHN:
 Fantasia 'No. 7' (Bèrben 1820) 59
 Farewell (Bèrben 2121) 60
 Forlorne Hope Fancy (Bèrben 2121) 61
 Fortune my Foe (Bèrben 2015) 62
 My Lord Willoby's Welcome Home (Zanibon 5579) 63
 Queen Elizabeth's Galliard (Bèrben 1935) 64
 Sir John Smith's Almaine (Bèrben 1592) 65
 Walsingham 66
DUARTE, JOHN WILLIAM:
 Alla Gavotta, Op. 21 (Columbia 183) 67
 All in a Row, Op. 51 (Bèrben 1971) 1st movement 68
 Birds, Op. 66 (Tuscany Publications) Sparrows 69*a*
 Birds, Op. 66 (Tuscany Publications) Swallows 69*b*
 English Suite, Op. 31 (Novello) 1st movement 70*a*
 English Suite, Op. 31 (Novello) 2nd movement 70*b*
 Five Quiet Songs, Op. 37 (Bèrben 1520) The Birds 71
 A Flight of Fugues, Op. 44 (Broekmans 1015) No. 2 72*a*
 A Flight of Fugues, Op. 44 (Broekmans 1015) No. 3 72*b*
 Larghetto, Op. 4 (Columbia 1530) 73
 Mutations, Op. 58 (Bèrben 2042) Brahms 74*a*
 Mutations, Op. 58 (Bèrben 2042) Bird Song 74*b*
 Prelude, Canto and Toccata, Op. 38 (Bèrben 1419) Canto 75
 Prélude en Arpèges, Op. 62 (Eschig 8213) 76
 Simple Prelude, Op. 19 (Guitar Review No. 17) 77
 Six Easy Pictures, Op. 56 (Novello) The Clock 78*a*
 Six Easy Pictures, Op. 56 (Novello) Lullaby 78*b*
 Some of Noah's Ark, Op. 55 (Ricordi LD 583) The Cuckoo 79*a*
 Some of Noah's Ark, Op. 55 (Ricordi LD 583) The Snake 79*b*
 Sonatina, Op. 27 (Casa de la Guitarra) 1st movement 80*a*
 Sonatina, Op. 27 (Casa de la Guitarra) 2nd movement 80*b*
 Sonatina, Op. 27 (Casa de la Guitarra) 3rd movement 80*c*
 Sonatina Lirica, Op. 48 (Bèrben 1972) 1st movement 81*a*
 Sonatina Lirica, Op. 48 (Bèrben 1972) 2nd movement 81*b*
 Sonatinette, Op. 35 (Novello) 1st movement 82*a*
 Sonatinette, Op. 35 (Novello) 2nd movement 82*b*
 Sonatinette, Op. 35 (Novello) 3rd movement 82*c*
 Sua Cosa, Op. 52 (Bèrben 2043) 83
 Suite Ancienne, Op. 47 (Bèrben 2203) Gigue 84*a*
 Suite Ancienne, Op. 47 (Bèrben 2203) Sarabande 84*b*
 Suite Piemontese, Op. 46 (Bèrben 1514) Canzona 85*a*
 Suite Piemontese, Op. 46 (Bèrben 1514) Danza 85*b*
 Tout en Ronde, Op. 57 (Universal 29153) Ritual Dance 86*a*
 Tout en Ronde, Op. 57 (Universal 29153) Spring Dance 86*b*
 Tout en Ronde, Op. 57 (Universal 29153) Waltz 86*c*
 Variations on a Catalan Folksong, Op. 25 (Novello) 87
ELGAR, SIR EDWARD:
 Enigma Variations, theme (Novello) 88
FARNABY, GILES:
 Tower Hill (Schott 10988) 89
FINK, SIEGFRIED:
 Dialoge for guitar and percussion (Zimmermann 1835) 90
FERRABOSCO, ALFONSO:
 Galliard 91

FILIPPI, AMADEO DE:
 Galliarde (Eschig) 92
FOX, VICTOR:
 Prelude, Hymn and Allegro (Bèrben 1644) Prelude 93
FRANCK, CESAR:
 Quasi Lento (Schott GA 118) 94
FRESCOBALDI, GIROLAMO:
 Corrente (Schott GA 158) 95
GIULIANI, MAURO:
 Divertissement, Op. 78/4 96
 Giulianate, Op. 148/1 97
 Grande Ouverture, Op. 61 98
 Leçon, Op. 51/7 99
 Mes fleurs Choisies, Op. 46/4, Le Jasmin 100
 Rondo, Op. 14/5 101
 Rossiniana No. 1, Op. 119 102
 Study, Op. 1/2 103
 Study, Op. 1/4 104
 Study, Op. 1/7 105
 Study, Op. 1/10 106
 Study, Op. 48/23 107
 Variations, Op. 112 (Suvini Zerboni 7764) 108
 Variations. Op. 142 (Suvini Zerboni 7727) 109
HANDEL, GEORGE FREDERICK:
 Aria 'Art Thou Troubled?' 110
 Minuet 111
 Messiah, 'And With His Stripes' 112
 Sarabande (Schott GA 148) 113
HAUG, HANS:
 Alba (Bèrben 1480) 114
HAYDN, FRANZ, JOSEPH:
 Minuet (Schott GA 139) 115
HOLBORNE, ANTONY:
 Pavan (Bèrben 2090) 116
 Untitled Piece (Bèrben 1725) 117
KARGEL, SIXTUS:
 Fantasia I, 1574 118
LEGNANI, LUIGI;
 Variations, Op. 224 (Schott GA 74) 119
MARTIN, FRANK:
 Quatre Pièces Brèves (Universal 12711) Air 120
MILAN, LUIS:
 Fantasia I (Suvini Zerboni/Chiesa, all Milan items) 121
 Fantasia IV 122
 Fantasia VII 123
 Fantasia IX 124
 Fantasia X 125
 Fantasia XV 126
 Fantasia XVII 127
 Fantasia XX 128
 Fantasia XXVII 129
 Fantasia XXX 130
 Fantasia XXXIV 131
 Pavanas III 132
 Pavanas IV 133
 Pavanas V 134
 Tentos III 135
MILANO, FRANCESCO CANOVA DA:
 Fantasia I (Suvini Zerboni/Chiesa all items) 136
 Fantasia XXV 137
 Fantasia XXVII 138
 Ricercare I 139
 Ricercare V 140
 Ricercare XIII 141
 Ricercare XVI 142

Ricercare XXI	143	
Ricercare XXVIII	144	
Ricercare XXXIV	145	
Ricercare LIV	146	
Ricercare LIX	147	

MORLAYE, GUILLAUME:

Fantaisie I	148

MORLEY, THOMAS:

Pavan (Bèrben 2090)	149

MOZART, W.A.:

Andante, K487 (Universal 11461)	150
Minuet K94 (Schott 11081)	151
Minuet (Schott GA 117)	152

MUDARRA, ALONSO DE:

Gallarda (Schott GA 176)	153

NARVAEZ, LUYS DE:

Cancion de l'Emperador (Schott GA 176)	154

NORMAN, THEODORE:

Exit (Schirmer 45408)	155

PEDRELL, CARLOS:

Página Romantica (Schott GA 120)	156

PONCE, MANUEL MARIA:

Preludes (GA 124) No. 1	157
Preludes (GA 124) No. 2	158
Preludes (GA 124) No. 3	159
Preludes (GA 124) No. 5	160
Preludes (GA 125) No. 8	161
Preludes (GA 125) No. 10	162
Preludes (GA 125) No. 11	163
Preludes (GA 125) No. 12	164
Sonata III (Schott GA 110) 2nd movement	165
Sonata Clásica (Schott GA 122) 1st movement	166
Sonata Romantica (Schott GA 123) 1st movement	167a
Sonata Romantica (Schott GA 123) 4th movement	167b
Sonatina Meridional (Schott GA 151) 1st movement	168
Thème Varié et Finale (Schott GA 109)	169
Valse (Schott GA 153)	170
Variations and Fugue on Las Folias (Schott GA 135)	171

PUJOL, EMILIO:

Tango (Eschig 1204)	172

RAMEAU, JEAN-PHILIPPE:

Minuet (Schott GA 160)	173

RAVEL, MAURICE:

Pavane pour une Infante Défunte (Schott GA 494)	174

REUSNER, ESAIAS:

Sonatina (Universal 29157)	175

RODRIGO, JOAQUIN:

Pequeña Sevillana (Ediciones Joaquin Rodrigo 190127)	176

ROSETTA, GIUSEPPE:

Canti della Pianura (Bèrben 1813) Mattutino	177
Mirage (Bèrben 1719)	178
Sei Poemi Brevi (Bèrben 1720) Burlesca	179a
Sei Poemi Brevi (Bèrben 1720) Cancion da Cuna	179b
Sei Poemi Brevi (Bèrben 1720) Nocturno	179c

SANZ, GASPAR:

Gallarda	180
Passacalles	181

SANTORSOLA, GUIDO:

Sonata No. 2 'Hispanica' (Bèrben 1722) 1st movement	182a
Sonata No. 2 'Hispanica' (Bèrben 1722) 2nd movement	182b
Sonata No. 2 'Hispanica' (Bèrben 1722) Finale	182c

SCARLATTI, DOMENICO:

Sonata K318/L31 (Schott GA 228)	183
Sonata K322/L483 (Bèrben 1777)	184
Sonata K334/L100	185

SCHUBERT, FRANZ:

Heidenröslein (Bèrben 1819)	186
Tod und das Mädchen (Bèrben 1819)	187

SOR, FERNANDO:

Fantaisie Op. 7 (Suvini Zerboni 7890)	188
Sonata Op. 22 Minuet	189
Sonata Op. 25 (Ricordi BA/9600) 1st movement	190a
Sonata Op. 25 (Ricordi BA/9600) Minuet	190b
Study, Op. 6/2	191
Study, Op. 6/3 (Segovia No. 11)	192
Study, Op. 6/6 (Segovia No. 12)	193
Study, Op. 6/8 (Segovia No. 1)	194
Study, Op. 6/9 (Segovia No. 13)	195
Study, Op. 6/12 (Segovia No. 14)	196
Study, Op. 29/1 (Segovia No. 19)	197
Study, Op. 29/2	198
Study, Op. 29/10 (Segovia No. 18)	199
Study, Op. 31/4	200
Study, Op. 31/14	201
Study, Op. 31/20 (Segovia No. 9)	202
Study, Op. 31/23	203
Study, Op. 35/1	204
Study, Op. 35/2	205
Study, Op. 35/3	206
Study, Op. 35/4	207
Study, Op. 35/6	208
Study, Op. 35/9	209
Study, Op. 35/11	210
Study, Op. 35/13 (Segovia No. 2)	211
Study, Op. 35/20	212
Study, Op. 35/21	213
Study, Op. 35/22 (Segovia No. 5)	214
Study, Op. 60/10	215
Study, Op. 60/13	216
Study Sor/Coste in C major	217
Study Sor/Coste in A minor	218a
Study Sor/Coste in E minor	218b
Variations 'Theme of Mozart', Op. 9	219
Variations Op. 26	220

SPINACINO, FRANCESCO:

Ricercare (Suvini Zerboni 6892)	221

STOKER, RICHARD:

Sonatina (Bèrben 1978) 1st movement	222

TANSMAN, ALEXANDRE:

Cavatina (Schott GA 165) Preludio	223a
Cavatina (Schott GA 165) Sarabande	223b
Danza Pomposa (Schott GA 206)	224
Suite in Modo Polonico (Eschig) Alla Polacca	225a
Suite in Modo Polonico (Eschig) Berceuse d'Orient	225b
Suite in Modo Polonico (Eschig) Entrée	225c
Suite in Modo Polonico (Eschig) Rêverie	225d

TÁRREGA, FRANCISCO:

Adelita	226
Alborada	227
Capricho Arabe	228
Maria	229
Prelude No. 2	230
Prelude No. 5	231

TÓRROBA, FEDERICO MORENO:

Burgalesa (Schott GA 113)	232
Los Mayos (Schott GA 134)	233
Nocturno (Schott GA 103)	234
Sonata Burlesca (Schott GA 115)	235

Sonatina (Columbia 1680) 1st movement	236*a*
Sonatina (Columbia 1680) 2nd movement	236*b*
Suite Castellana (Schott GA 104) Arada	237*a*
Suite Castellana (Schott GA 104) Danza	237*b*

TRADITIONAL (BRITISH):

Adeste Fideles	238
Bushes and Briars	239
Drink to me only	240
God Save the Queen	241
Good King Wenceslas	242
Goodnight Ladies	243
Lass of Richmond Hill	244
Little Brown Jug	245
Matthew, Mark, Luke and John	246
Sailors' Hornpipe	247
Tarry Trowsers	248
The First Nowell	249
The Lark in the Morning	250
The Vicar of Bray	251
There is a Tavern in the Town	252
Three Blind Mice	253
What Shall we do with the Drunken Sailor?	254

(CATALAN):

La Fille del Marxant (arr. Llobet)	255

(FRENCH):

J'ai du Bon Tabac	256
Quand Trois Poules	257

(GERMAN):

Hymn: *Aus tiefer Noth*	258

(HEBRIDEAN):

Skye boat song	259

(IRISH):

The Next Market Day	260

(WELSH):

David of the White Rock	261
The Ash Grove	262

TURINA, JOAQUIN:

Fandanguillo (Schott GA 102)	263
Hommage à Tárrega (Schott GA 136)	264
Ráfaga (Schott GA 128)	265

VILLA-LOBOS, HEITOR:

Preludes (Eschig) No. 2	266
Preludes (Eschig) No. 3	267
Preludes (Eschig) No. 5	268

VISÉE, ROBERT DE:

Suite IX in D minor, Gigue	269*a*
Suite IX in D minor, Sarabande	269*b*

WEISS, SYLVIUS LEOPOLD:

(London) Suite No. IX (Chiesa/Suvini Zerboni) Allemande	270
(London) Suite No. XI, Sarabande	271
Tombeau sur la Mort de M. Cajetan (Broekmans 1286)	272

WILLS, ARTHUR:

Galliard (Ricordi LD 615)	273

WISSMER, PIERRE:

Partita (Bèrben 1518) Preludio	274

APPENDIX II

Key to Musical Examples

Example	Reference	Example	Reference	Example	Reference
1a)	245	b)	110	b)	6 *a*
b)	251	c)	191	c)	269 *a*
c)	244	d)	186	d)	115
d)	262	e)	242	33a)	270
e)	243	f)	261	b)	52
f)	240	g)	26	c)	203
2b)	259	h)	242	d)	4
3	252	23	88	e)	118
10a)	248	24a)	95	34a)	240
b)	260	b)	237 *a*	b)	63
c)	258	c)	167 *b*	c)	66
d)	239	d)	204	d)	25
e)	250	25	44 *b*	35	253
11a)	57	26a)	109	36	257
b)	21	b)	112	37	214
c)	22	c)	67	38a)	185
d)	140	d)	7	b)	11
e)	54	e)	73	c)	151
12a)	80 *b*	27a)	177	39	190 *b*
b)	80 *b*	b)	164	40a)	226
c)	225 *a*	28a)	219	b)	254
d)	225 *d*	b)	180	c)	71
e)	170	29a,b)	62	d)	80 *b*
f)	225 *b*	c)	189	e)	187
g)	81 *b*	d)	3 *b*	43a)	124
h)	225 *c*	e)	64	b)	126
15a)	121	f)	256	c)	122
b)	122	30a)	89	d)	133
c)	123	b)	158	e)	131
d)	129	c)	157	44a)	141
	135	d)	16 *a*	b)	136
e)	132	e)	173	c)	142
f)	132	f)	206	d)	143
16a)	53	g)	247	55	204
b)	118	h)	10	56	204
17a)	122	i)	97	57	106
b)	60	31a)	246	65 Authentic	
19	153	b)	269 *b*	a)	210
20a)	227	c)	115	b)	216
b)	228	d)	162	c)	205
22a)	241	e)	77	d)	206
	184	32a)	183	e)	100

154

Example	Reference	Example	Reference	Example	Reference
f)	101	85a)	220	102a)	3 a
g)	107	b)	102	b)	207
h)	106	c)	2	c)	6 b
i)	103	d)	167 a	d)	41
j)	96	e)	163	103a)	189
k)	40	86a)	24	c)	40
l)	147	b)	51	104a)	163
m)	146	c)	192	b)	170
n)	134	d)	119	105	251
o)	125	89a)	6 c	106a)	189
p)	223 a	b)	52	b)	8
q)	223 b		59	c)	266
r)	176	c)	47	107	171
Plagal			153	111a)	169
a)	154		33	b)	169
b)	60	d)	127	c)	169
c)	128		53	d)	184
d)	130		221	e)	120
e)	138		139	f)	197
f)	137		175	g)	171
g)	144		55	h)	232
h)	145	e)	148	i)	171
i)	94		149	j)	224
j)	160		91	m)	263
k)	233	f)	194	n)	82 b
l)	82 b	g)	43	o)	234
68b)	99		12	p)	113
70a)	35		195	q)	168
b)	211	92a)	111	r)	13
c)	104		242	s)	17
d)	11	95a)	201	t)	19 a
71a)	42	b)	113	112a)	44 a
b)	214	c)	113	b)	171
c)	105	98a)	19 b	113a)	179 b
d)	152	b)	198	b)	171
e)	271	99a)	5	c)	268
72a)	115	b)	193	115	16 b
b)	19 b	c)	181	116a)	171
c)	272	d)	23	b)	87
73a)	15	e)	48	c)	84 b
74	162	f)	34	118a)	234
75	241	100a)	56	119a)	16 b
76	238	b)	39	b)	188
78	262	101	150	c)	36

Example	Reference	Example	Reference	Example	Reference
120a)	76	134a)	28	d)	31
b)	197	b)	1 b	e)	171
121a)	214	c)	27	148a)	231
b)	50	136a)	45 f	b)	45 h
c)	9 b	b)	233	c)	84 a
122a)	202	c)	80 c	d)	171
b)	9 a	d)	203	e)	80 c
c)	194	e)	80 a	f)	162
d)	11	f)	28	g)	159
e)	196	g)	86 b	150a)	218 b
f)	49	h)	178	b)	223 a
g)	214	i)	156	c)	211
h)	50	137a)	117	d)	229
i)	209	b)	50	e)	228
j)	213	c)	218 a	f)	84 b
k)	199	d)	194	g)	38
l)	212	e)	237 b	h)	14 b
127a)	80 a	f)	190 a	153a)	200
b)	80 a	g)	14 a	b)	108
c)	80 a	h)	217	c)	37
128	179 b	i)	65	d)	108
129a)	1 a	j)	116	e)	70 a
b)	174	k)	236 b	f)	70 b
130a)	80 c	l)	80 a	g)	45 c
b)	80 a	140a)	197	h)	36
c)	80 c	b)	115	i)	45 g
d)	179 a	c)	167 b	j)	108
132a)	174	d)	165	k)	236 a
b)	83	e)	169	l)	190 a
c)	93	141a)	45 a	m)	161
d)	93	b)	45 b	154a)	45 e
e)	86 c	c)	81 b	b)	45 e
f)	174	142	46	c)	45 e
133a)	81 a	143	79 b	155a)	61
b)	211	144	79 a	b)	61
c)	175	145a)	265	c)	60
d)	45 b	b)	74 b	d)	60
e)	171	c)	263	e)	45 b
f)	174	d)	235	f)	81 b
g)	80 a	e)	79 a	g)	86 a
h)	232	146a)	172	156a)	98
i)	20	b)	81 b	b)	166
j)	222	c)	86 c	c)	45 g
				d)	87

Example	Reference	Example	Reference
e)	230	d)	29
f)	172	e)	29
g)	171	165a)	68
h)	171	b)	68
i)	85 a	c)	155
j)	70 b	d)	90
157a)	211	e)	182 a
b)	45 b	f)	182 a
c)	78 b	g)	182 a
d)	255	h)	182 b
e)	237 a	i)	182 b
f)	74 a	j)	182 b
g)	58	k)	182 c
h)	18		
i)	204		
j)	208		
k)	208		
l)	72 b		
158a)	82 a		
b)	82 a		
c)	82 c		
d)	45 d		
e)	45 d		
f)	92		
g)	32		
h)	273		
159a)	69 b		
b)	69 a		
c)	30		
160a)	85 b		
161a)	179 c		
b)	114		
c)	274		
d)	225 b		
162a)	46		
b)	46		
c)	267		
d)	266		
163a)	78 a		
b)	75		
c)	72 a		
164a)	79 a		
b)	75		
c)	29		

FURTHER READING

The enterprising reader may find the following (far from comprehensive) list interesting. Inevitably, many of their musical examples will be impossible to play on the guitar (or playable only after adaptation) and working through them will be slower and more difficult. Within such a vast and complex subject the reader may not be surprised to find differences, and even contradictions, from one book to another; some may be dismayed by these, others stimulated.

Burnard, David Alexander: *Harmony and Composition for the Student and Potential Composer* (Angus & Robertson, o.p.)

Butterworth, Anna: *Harmony in Practice* (Associated Board of the Royal Schools of Music)

Cole, Hugo: *Sounds and Signs: Aspects of Musical Notation* (Oxford)

Gavall, John: *Learning Music through the Guitar,* 5 vols (Belwin Mills)

Hindemith, Paul: *The Craft of Musical Composition,* 2 vols (Schott)

Jeans, Sir James: *Science and Music* (Dover)

Karkoschka, Erhard: *Notation in New Music* (Universal)

Macpherson, Stewart: *Melody and Harmony* Books 1, 2, and 3 (Stainer and Bell)

Persichetti, Vincent: *Twentieth-Century Harmony* (Faber)

Piston, Walter: *Harmony* (Gollancz)

Siegmeister, Elie: *Harmony and Melody,* 2 vols (Wadsworth)

Smith Brindle, Reginald: *The New Music* (Oxford)

Smith Brindle, Reginald: *Serial Composition* (Oxford)

Spencer, Peter: *The Practice of Harmony* (Prentice Hall)

Toch, Ernst: *The Shaping Forces in Music* (Dover)

The Oxford Harmony: Vol. 1 (R.O. Morris), Vol. 2 (H.K. Andrews) (Oxford)

CHORDS AND THEIR INVERSIONS: ANSWERS (see p. 53)

Ex. 46 – R. Ex. 47 – R, R. Ex. 48 – R. Ex. 49(*a*) I, (*b*) R.

Ex. 50 – R, I, II, R, I, II. Ex. 51 – R, R, I, I, II, II. Ex. 52 – all R. Ex. 53 – all R.

INDEX

Added Ninth, Chords of 107
Added Sixth, Chords of 93
Aleatory Composition 149
Appoggiatura – Chord 74
              Notes 68
Atonality 145
Augmented Sixth, Chords of 125
Augmented Triad 75, 115
Authentic – Cadences 61
          Modes 16
Auxiliary Notes 69
Binary Form 43
Bitonality 143
Byetones 68
Cadences – Amen 61
         Authentic 60
         Deceptive 65
         Direct 63
         Feminine 74
         Full-close 60
         Half-close 60
         Imperfect 60
         Indirect 63
         Interrupted 65
         Masculine 74
         Melodic 42
         Pathetic 123
         Perfect 60
         Plagal 60
         Six-four 64
         Surprise 65
Cadential Six-four 64
Campanile Effect 139
Changing Notes 35
Characteristic Notes 52
Chords – Added Ninth 107
       Added Sixth 93
       Appoggiatura 73
       Augmented Sixth 125
       Augmented Triad 75
       Clusters 139
       Common 50
       Definition of 47
       Diminished Fifth 118
       Diminished Seventh 98
       Diminished Triad 75
       Dominant of Dominant 83
       Dominant Ninth 103
       Dominant Seventh 69
       Dominant Triad 56
       Eleventh 110
       Fourths, Built from 137
       French Sixth 125
       German Sixth 125
       Gratuitous Dissonances 139
       Italian Sixth 125
       Leading Sevenths 97
       Major Leading Seventh 97
       Major Triad 50
       Minor Triad 50
       Neapolitan Sixth 123
       Nexus 83
       Pivot 83
       Progressions of 59
       Secondary Ninths 106
       Secondary Sevenths 89
       Secondary Sevenths in Minor Mode .. 94
       Secondary Triads 75
       Thirteenth 110
Cluster Chords 139
Comma of Pythagoras 7
Chromatic – Alteration of Diatonic Chords 115
         Harmony 120
         Harmony Arising From
         Part-Movement 128
         Scale 28
Circle of Keys (Fifths) 59
Common – Chords 50
         Notes 59
Conjunct Motion 40
Consonance and Dissonance 47
Deceptive Cadence 65
Diminished Seventh Chord 98
Diminished Triad 75
Disjunct Motion 40
Dodecaphony 146
Dominant – of The Dominant 83
         of a Mode 15
         Pedals 136
         Ninth Chord 103
         Seventh Chord 69
         Triad 56
Dorian Sixth 66
Eleventh, Chords of 110
Essential Notes 68
Expedient Notation 98
False Relations 26
Figured Bass 57
Flattened (Diminished) Fifth, Chords With 118
Fourths, Chords Built From 137
French Sixth, Chord 125
Full-Close – Embellishment of 72
         Harmonic 60
         Melodic 43
Functional Symbols of Chords 57
Fundamental Note 5
German Sixth, Chord 125
Gratuitous Dissonances 139
Gruppetto 35
Half-Close – Harmonic 64
         Melodic 43
Harmonic (= Partial, Overtone) 5
Induced Harmony 68
Interrupted Cadence 65
Intervals – Character of 47
         Consonance of 47
         Harmonic Effect of 47
Inversions of Triads, Aural Effect of 51
Italian Sixth, Chord 125
Key, Changing of 13
Leading and Leaning notes 21
Leading Seventh Chords 97
Magadizing 49
Major – Leading Seventh Chord 97
         Seventh Chord 90
         Triad 50
Masculine/Feminine Cadences 74

Melody	– Cadences and Climaxes in	42
	Curves of	44
	Full-/Half-closes in	43
	Motifs in	37
	Scalic Tendencies in	29
	Sequences in	36
Minor	– Seventh Chord	90
	Triad	50
	Major Seventh Chord	94
Modes	– Authentic	16
	Decay of	21
	Dominant of	16
	Final of	16
	Identity of	15
	Mixed	17
	Plagal	16
Modulating Sequences		85
Modulation	– Definition of	81
	Extraneous (Remote)	82, 88, 131
	Simple (Close)	81
	to Dominant Key	82
	to Mediant Key	85
	to Subdominant Key	82
	to Submediant Key	83
	to Supertonic Key	84
Motifs, in Melody		37
Musica Ficta		21
Musique Concrète		4
Neapolitan Sixth, Chord		123
Nexus Chords		83
Ninth	– Chords of Added	107
	Dominant	103
	Secondary	106
Note Cambiate		35
Note Row		145
Organum		49
Oscillation		4
Overtone (= Harmonic, Partial)		5
Pantonality		143
Parallel Harmony		141
Partial (= Harmonic, Overtone)		5
Passing Notes		68
Pathetic Cadence		123
Pedal Points		134
Perfect Cadences		60
Pitch, Standardisation of		6
Pivot Chords		83
Plagal	– Cadence	60
	Modes	16
Polytonality		143
Primary	– Seventh Chord	69
	Triads	66
Progressions of Chords		59
Pythagoras, Comma of		7
Ragas		17
Root	– of a Chord	51
	Progressions	60
Scales	– Chromatic	28
	Diatonic	15
	Gapped	11
	Heptatonic	11
	Major	11
	Minor	15
	Modal	15
	Pentatonic	11
	Whole-Tone	28

Secondary	– Ninth Chords	106
	Seventh Chords	89
	Triads	75
Sequences	– Melodic	36
	Modulating	85
Serial Composition		146
Seventh Chords	– Diminished	98
	Dominant	69
	Leading	97
	Major Leading	97
	Primary	69
	Secondary Major	89
	Secondary Minor	94
Signum Asinorum		21
Sixth Chords	– Added	93
	Augmented	125
	French	125
	German	125
	Italian	125
	Neapolitan	123
Subdominant Triad		56
Surprise Cadence		65
Suspensions		69
Symbolization of Chords –		
	Alfabeto	57
	Chord Symbols	57
	Figured Bass	57
	Functional	56
Temperament		8
Thirteenth Chords		110
Tierce de Picardie		50
Tonality	– Atonality	145
	Bitonality	143
	Nature of	140
	Negation of	145
	Pantonality	143
	Polytonality	143
	Undermining of	140
Tonic	– Chord	51
	Note	12
	Pedal	136
Total Serialization		146
Transition		81
Transposition		13
Triads	– Augmented	75, 115
	Characteristic Note of	52
	Direct/Indirect	53
	Diminished	75
	Dominant	56
	Inversions of	51
	Major and Minor	50
	Primary	66
	Root of	51
	Secondary	75
	Stability of	55
	Subdominant	56
	Substitution of Primary	76
Tritone (*Diabolus in Musica, Quinta Falsa*)		25
Twelve-Note Composition		145
Unessential Notes		68
Vibration	– Amplitude of	4
	Cycle of	4
	Loops and Nodes of	5
	Overtone Series	6
Vibration	– of Strings	4
Voice-Leading		59
Whole-Tone Scale		28

160